WALKING WI...
DAILY D...
PART
(July – Se...)

ISBN-13: 978-1-5120-9066-6
ISBN-10: 1-5120-9066-2

"The anointed Word
will set you free"

Published by Springs International

AAB '2015

DEDICATION

This book is dedicated to all those
who are genuinely seeking to grow up spiritually.

CONTENTS

WHY I WROTE THIS BOOK

**And Enoch walked with God; and he *was* not,
for God took him.** – Genesis 5:24

16 years ago, I was in my final days as an undergraduate at one of the top universities in my country of birth. My graduating class at the Electronic & Electrical Engineering Department had organised a yearbook, where each of us was assigned a page to talk about our school experiences and future aspirations. I remember one of the questions asked was: *Who is your role model?* After a careful consideration, I wrote down this answer: *Enoch, who walked with God, and was not, for God took him.*

I had been fascinated by this man: *Enoch*, who walked far ahead of his time, and I had made up my mind not to settle for less, especially when I understood that, by being *born-again*, I had come into a *personal relationship* with God through Jesus Christ, my Lord and Saviour. The interesting part was to find out that *walking with God is simple* (I didn't say easy!). I found that walking with God is a choice, and all it requires is: *attention, diligence and perseverance*.

In many years of experience as a spiritual mentor, I have come to find out that many Christians are not paying attention to the Word. Many don't read their bible daily while others struggle to understand what they have read. This is why I wrote this book in obedience to God's leading. *I wrote it for you!* This devotional will help to *fast-track* your understanding of divine truths. However, you have the responsibility of reading it daily and applying the truths revealed therein. This book will *complement* your daily Bible study. My passionate desire is that you will walk with God, grow up spiritually, and live victoriously! Be blessed.

Ben AAB Awoseyila

HOW TO USE THIS DEVOTIONAL

This book is simple and easy-to-read. However, the first thing you need to do is: **make a decision to never miss a day's reading**, no matter how busy you are. This will help you to make the most of this devotional.

OPENING:
This book includes a **victory confession** and a **victory prayer** at its beginning. Try to **say these out** every day or as often as you can, before reading the day's devotional.

BASIC READING:
Start by **saying out** the scripture verses of the day. Then **read** the accompanying teaching of the day patiently. Finally, **say out** the prayer or confession of the day.

ADVANCED READING:
In addition to the steps listed for basic reading, you should seek to **memorise** the scripture verses of the day. Furthermore, you should **open up** the scripture references within the day's text, for further study and meditation.

GROUP STUDY:
For group study, **all the elements of the basic and advanced reading** should be incorporated. It is very important to provide an atmosphere of **balanced discussion** in group meetings. The leader should allow every member to **share their opinions** regarding the chosen topic and to **ask relevant questions**. The discussion can be further enriched by using **other scripture verses** relevant to the topic. The group leader shall take overall responsibility of **guiding the discussion** and **making conclusions** based on the truths revealed by the Word.

VICTORY CONFESSION

My Bible is the written Word of God.

The Word of God is true, alive and powerful.

I study and meditate on the Word.

I believe the Word.

I confess the Word.

I live by the Word.

I am what the Word says I am.

I can do what the Word says I can do.

The anointed Word will set me free.

Glory to God! Hallelujah! Amen!

VICTORY PRAYER

Dear Father in Heaven,

Grant me spiritual wisdom and revelation

in the knowledge of Jesus Christ.

Grant that the eyes of my heart be flooded with light.

Grant me to know the hope of your calling in me.

Grant me to know the riches of your glory in me.

Grant me to know the unlimited greatness of your power

in and for me.

I fervently ask for all these in Jesus' Name. Amen.

TOPICAL INDEX

July 1
THE GOOD SHEPHERD

The Lord *is* my shepherd; I shall not want. – Psalm 23:1

I am the good shepherd. The good shepherd gives His life for the sheep. – John 10:11

Many atheists criticise God because there exists suffering in this world. However, they are only looking for an excuse to live a selfish life that is not answerable to the divine will. Although suffering is the stark reality of this <u>fallen</u> world, God is not disconnected from our sufferings. *If you believe in God, then you don't have to suffer alone!* He's got you covered as *Jehovah Rohi: The Lord my Shepherd* (Psalm 23) The problem of suffering has been dealt with on the cross of Calvary. God Himself came down as Jesus Christ and took upon Himself our sin, sorrow, pain, sickness, disease and poverty. He became a curse for us, so that we can enjoy The BLESSING (Galatians 3:13). Jesus Christ is the Good Shepherd and <u>there is no other!</u> *If the Lord is your Shepherd, then what are you to Him?* Sheep are stupid because they follow, without doing much thinking of their own. However, they are not foolish because they know the voice of their Shepherd: *the voice of Wisdom!* Don't ever forget that God is for you and with you always. All you have to do is 'trust and obey'. *The Good Shepherd has given His life for the sheep.* It is now time for the sheep to make use of that life given (*Zoe: the divine overcoming life*) to live victoriously in this world through faith (John 10:10).

Prayer: *Heavenly Father, thank You because You are my Jehovah Rohi. You are my Shepherd and I am Your sheep. Therefore, I lack no good thing in life. You are my Lord. You are dominating my life. You are guiding and leading me.*

July 2
THE NEW BIRTH

But as many as received Him, to them He gave the right to become children of God, to those who believe in His name.
– John 1:12

When you believe that Jesus Christ is the Son of God, receive Him into your heart as the eternal sacrifice for your sins, and confess with your mouth that Jesus is your Lord, a supernatural event takes place. You become born-again, for *Life Infinite* (eternal life) comes into your darkened spirit (heart), thereby recreating it and restoring you into union and communion with God (Romans 10:9-10).

When you repent of your sins and trust in Christ Jesus as your Saviour and Lord, you instantly experience a *spiritual* birth into the kingdom of God. You're instantly delivered from the dominion of Satan and translated into the kingdom of Jesus Christ, which is full of *Life, Light and Love*. When you repent and receive the free gift of God, the blood of Jesus cleanses you from all unrighteousness and the Most High comes to dwell within you through His Holy Spirit. Notice that it is your spirit that gets born-again, for God gives you *a new heart* when you believe and receive Jesus. Your soul is progressively *renewed and sanctified* as you continue daily in studying the Word of God and prayer. Your body will be *glorified* at the resurrection (Rapture) of the saints. However, for now, you are to put your body *under the control* of your recreated spirit and present it as holy unto the Lord (John 3:6, Colossians 1:13-14).

Confession: I am a new creation in Christ Jesus. I am born of God and born by His Spirit. I am recreated in the image and likeness of God. Zoe, the life of God flows in me. I have God's nature of life, light and love within me. Hallelujah!

July 3
THE LAW OF FAITH

**So then faith comes by hearing,
and hearing by the word of God.** – Romans 10:17

In the natural life, we know that nothing gets done unless someone acts. For example, when you wake up at dawn, you may decide to either go back to sleep or to get up. The choice is yours and so are the consequences. The same principles apply spiritually, for we always reap what we sow, with the exception of mercy drops (Galatians 6:7). Why live on mercy drops when you have access by faith to the fullness of grace and truth; the fullness of divine life? *Faith is a spiritual law, just like the natural law of gravity. How faith works is not random and faith is not a wish list. The principles of faith are revealed throughout the Bible. They can be learned and mastered just like any other field of study.* The mere fact that you cannot perform a surgery does not mean that surgeons are 'lucky magicians' or that surgery is ineffective. If only you could apply yourself to enthusiastic study and persevering practice under guidance of accomplished surgeons, you will be able to make a success of it one day. The same process works with faith. *The greatest asset that God has given to every person is free will: the ability to make choices.* It is your responsibility to build yourself up in faith. You have the responsibility to believe the Word of God and to proclaim it over your situations. You are to claim your healing, supply, deliverance and victory by faith (Romans 3:27).

Prayer: *Dear Father, I thank You for the triumphant victory of Christ at the cross of Calvary. I rejoice that I can stand firm in that victory by faith. I refuse to be lazy. Help me to be a diligent student of the Word, in Jesus' Name. Amen.*

July 4
FAR FROM OPPRESSION

In righteousness you shall be established;
You shall be far from oppression, for you shall not fear;
And from terror, for it shall not come near you.
— Isaiah 54:14

There is a close connection between fear and oppression. *Fear opens the door to devil and fear opens the door to oppression!* When you worry about the unknown and you begin to fear what the future might bring your way, you are treading on dangerous ground. *Fear is the domain of the devil; he uses fear to torment and enslave those who are feeble-minded.* People living in fear never get to enjoy the best things that God has for them. Rather than staying their minds on Him (thereby enjoying His perfect peace), they focus on the possibilities and probabilities of evil. *The Bible says that you shall be far from oppression because you shall not fear. Yes, simply refuse to fear!* (Isaiah 26:3).

In order to defeat fear in your life, you need to be well established in righteousness and firmly rooted in love. Righteousness refers to a sense of right standing with God through our Lord Jesus Christ. This means that you are no longer a sinner or a stranger. Instead, you are now a fellow citizen with the saints, and a member of household of God (Ephesians 2:19). Righteousness also refers to allowing the life of God to dominate you in all you do. This involves walking by faith and walking in love. There is no fear in love but perfect love casts out fear (1 John 4:18).

Confession: *The Lord is my refuge and strength. He is my God in whom I trust. I simply refuse to fear. I am far from oppression because I fear no evil. The Lord is with me and I am established in His righteousness, in Jesus' Name. Amen.*

July 5
LOVE CASTS OUT FEAR

There is no fear in love; but perfect love casts out fear, because fear involves torment. But he who fears has not been made perfect in love. – 1 John 4:18

One of my favourite quotes from the Bible is in *1 John 4:18* which says that: 'there is no fear in love'. This also reminds me of another quote from *Proverbs 28:1* which says that 'the righteous are as bold as a lion'. *The combination of 'walking in love' and 'walking in righteousness' brings you into a state of optimum confidence in life.* This refers to a state where you hold nothing against anyone and you have nothing to be afraid of because you know that God is on your side. Love is the greatest commandment! *Loving the Lord your God with all your heart and soul and mind and strength is true worship: the whole purpose of your existence.* We are made and called to love (Mark 12:30).

The God-kind of love is not selfish human love that is based on returning favours. *It is a selfless overflowing love that is shed abroad in our hearts by the Holy Spirit.* This divine love becomes perfect (mature) as we allow it to blossom and dominate us completely. *People will offend and maltreat you!* Will that stop you from loving them again or loving others? *No! Perfect love casts out fear! When you're walking in love, the devil has nothing on you.* In this confidence, you can tell the devil to get lost when he shows up with disease or oppression. You say: *Satan, I'm walking in love. Take your hands off my life* (James 4:7)

Prayer: *Almighty God, I am privileged to call You my Father. Thank You for Your love nature that is inside of me. Help me to let it blossom. I refuse to be selfish! Help me to practise walking in divine love daily, in Jesus' Name. Amen.*

July 6
GOD IS LOVE

For God so loved the world that He gave His only begotten Son, that whoever believes in Him should not perish but have everlasting life. – John 3:16

The Most High is loving because that is His nature. *His love is compassion, not emotion; His love is not discriminatory.* God loves you and cares about you, irrespective of your background. He understands you beyond all others. He loves you because He made you and always desires the very best for you. God is gracious, benevolent and full of kindness. He acts to save. It was God's Love that necessitated the incarnation of the *eternal Word*. He literally came 'down to earth' to sacrifice Himself, in order to pay the universal and eternal price for Sin (1 John 4:8).
The Most High is patient with the sinner, forgives the repentant and also provides a way of escape from judgement. He causes His sun to shine on the good and the evil. He provides fresh air for the just and the unjust. His mercies are new every morning. However, God's mercy is His prerogative and cannot be taken for granted. God cannot break His Word and He cannot bless disobedience. Time will ultimately run out for those who refuse to take advantage of God's mercy (2 Corinthians 6:1-2).

**The LORD is gracious and full of compassion,
Slow to anger and great in mercy.**
– Psalm 145:8

Confession: The Most High is my eternal Father. He has loved me with an everlasting love. I now have eternal life dwelling in me because of His love. I have freely received God's love, and I will give it freely by walking in love daily.

July 7
GRIEVE NOT THE SPIRIT

And do not grieve the Holy Spirit of God, by whom you were sealed for the day of redemption.
– Ephesians 4:30

One of the symbols of the Holy Spirit is the dove. We see this illustrated in the life of Jesus Christ when He was baptised by *John the Baptist* and the Spirit descended upon Him like a dove, as recorded in *Mark 1:9-11. The dove represents gentleness, purity, peace and love.* This gives us an insight into the characteristics of the Holy Spirit in us. He is a sweet and gentle Spirit who usually leads us by the still small voice. He will not override our will, nor force us to do anything. *It is demons that force people to do things against their will.* The Holy Spirit nudges us gently from our inner man. Therefore, it is very important that we do not grieve the Spirit by habitually ignoring His promptings. *Those who practise 'having their way always' cannot please God.* Those who override the instructions of the Holy Spirit cannot grow up spiritually (Romans 8:5-8).

It is very important to stay in communion with the Holy Spirit and to practise a high sensitivity to His promptings. *Those who are led by the Spirit of God are the true sons of God.* Cultivate the habit of talking and listening to the Holy Spirit regularly. As you train your human spirit in practising the Word and obeying the inner guidance of the Spirit, you will be more accurate in being led by the Spirit. *Beware of disobedience, for it grieves the Spirit!* (Romans 8:14).

Prayer: *Heavenly Father, I thank You for sending Your precious Holy Spirit to dwell inside my heart. Help me to stay conscious of His presence and to commune with Him regularly. Help me to yield to His leading, in Jesus' Name.*

July 8
HELP FROM WITHIN

Likewise the Spirit also helps in our weaknesses. For we do not know what we should pray for as we ought, but the Spirit Himself makes intercession for us with groanings which cannot be uttered. – Romans 8:26

The primary ministry of the Holy Spirit in the life of true believers is to help us become everything that God has called us to be. He is our Divine Helper! *Your primary weakness as a believer is your inability to pray as you ought to.* Most of us struggle with prayer because of our fleshly nature. The untrained flesh is interested in pleasure and entertainment, but when it comes to prayer, it usually loves to *back off.* Moreover, even when we begin to pray, our mind takes over, and before we know it, we have run of out steam and ideas. That is where the help of the Holy Spirit comes in. *He has come to inspire and empower you to pray appropriately and effectively.* He lives in you, so as to take hold with you in prayer, as you yield to him by praying in the Spirit (Jude 20, 1 Corinthians 14:2,14).

The Holy Spirit does not pray for us while we fold back our hands doing nothing. No! He prays with us through us. He makes intercession for us through words which cannot be articulated in human language. These words are called 'unknown tongues'. He inspires us to pray in tongues, making our prayers spirit-to-Spirit, in line with the will of God. We pray in the Spirit <u>by faith</u> and God understands what the Spirit is speaking through us (Romans 8:27).

Confession: I have the Spirit of the living God dwelling in me. I choose to be full of the Word and full of the Spirit. I drink of the Spirit by speaking in tongues. I pray and sing with tongues to release the supernatural upon my world.

July 9
THE WORD IS TRUTH

Sanctify them by Your truth. Your word is truth
– John 17:17

Many people like to be realistic. This usually means that they like to live by the facts of the day. However, they forget that facts change because facts are temporal in nature. In contrast, Truth is absolute and unchanging. Truth is *the written Word* of God (the Bible). Truth is a person: Jesus Christ of Nazareth (also known as *the Living Word*). God created the world by His Word, and upholds all things by His Word. *The Word of God contains the true realities of life*. These realities include salvation, healing, deliverance and provision. The Word of God supersedes facts and changes facts. The Word of God is forever settled in Heaven (John 1:3, Hebrews 1:3, Psalm 119:89).

It is only the Truth you know that has the power to set you free. This refers to 'revelation knowledge' which comes by abiding in His Word. *Things of value do not come cheap*. To enjoy the benefits of the Word, you have to let it dominate your life completely. This comes by studying, meditating, believing, confessing and practising the Word. The Word of God is full of life and it is certain that *the anointed Word will set you free* (Hosea 4:6, Psalm 119:105, James 1:22).

Then Jesus said to those Jews who believed Him, "If you abide in My word, you are My disciples indeed. And you shall know the truth, and the truth shall make you free." – John 8:31-32

Prayer: *Dear Father in Heaven, thank You for Your precious holy written Word. I am sorry for taking Your Word lightly. I will allow the Word to dominate me totally. I will study, meditate, confess and obey the Word daily, in Jesus' Name.*

July 10
ADMIT YOUR FAULTS

Confess *your* trespasses to one another, and pray for one another, that you may be healed. – James 5:16

A major symptom of pride is the inability to admit one's fault. *People don't want to be judged, yet they are so quick to judge others!* We need to get one thing clear: being instructed and corrected is not the same thing as being judged. When Jesus said 'judge not', He was referring to the self-righteous condemnation of others. *Indeed, we should avoid destructive criticism*. However, there is room for correction and rebuke. You cannot go far in your walk with God if you are unwilling to admit your faults and take correction from others (Galatians 6:1, Proverbs 15:31-33).
Nobody is permanently wrong and no one is permanently right, for we all make mistakes! Therefore, 'admitting your fault and saying sorry' is one of the most important things you will learn to do on this side of eternity. *Admitting your faults has to do with humility and maturity*. Admitting your fault and saying sorry reflects repentance towards God and men. *A major hindrance to healing and answered prayer is the lack of repentance*. That is why the Bible says that you should confess your faults and pray, so that you may be healed. This refers to the importance of repentance in connection with living victoriously. Don't sweep your faults under the carpet. Instead, admit, confess and forsake them, so as to obtain mercy and grace. *Admitting your faults helps you to mature* (Proverbs 28:13, Hebrews 4:16).

Confession: I am a child of God. I live in His righteousness. I refuse to be proud and stubborn. I embrace a lifestyle of quick repentance. I am willing to admit my faults and say sorry whenever I'm wrong. Glory to God! Hallelujah! Amen!

July 11
SUPPORT YOUR PASTOR

Let the elders who rule well be counted worthy of double honor, especially those who labor in the word and doctrine. For the Scripture says, "You shall not muzzle an ox while it treads out the grain," and, "The laborer *is* worthy of his wages." – 1 Timothy 5:17-18

In *Genesis 12:3*, God said to Abraham that He would bless those who blessed him and curse those who cursed him. This must be so, because God had chosen that in Abraham shall all nations be blessed. *The way to maintain a vital flow of blessing is to stay well-connected to the channel of blessing.* Your Pastor is your God-appointed channel of divine blessing. *He is your spiritual elder and father.* Count him worthy of double honour. Hold him in high esteem for his work's sake (1 Thessalonians 5:12-13).

Supporting your Pastor is not optional, for the labourer is worthy of his wages. When you bless the 'man of God' with your earthly possessions, God will bless you in those areas of need that are beyond your power. This is a divine principle as revealed in the story of *Elijah and the widow of Zarephath* (1 Kings 17). Just as the body cannot do without the head, so also the head cannot do without the body. Your Pastor needs your continuous *spiritual, moral and financial support* in order to fulfil the vision given by God. Every good thing you do to support and encourage your Pastor is credited to your Heavenly account. *Supporting your Pastor is part of your service to God* (Galatians 6:6-7).

Prayer: *Almighty and Everlasting God, I rededicate myself to You: spirit, soul and body. I refuse to be proud and selfish. I choose to be obedient to the Word! Help me to support my Pastor in every possible way, in Jesus' Name.*

July 12
HIMSELF TOOK IT

When evening had come, they brought to Him many who were demon-possessed. And He cast out the spirits with a word, and healed all who were sick, that it might be fulfilled which was spoken by Isaiah the prophet, saying: "He Himself took our infirmities And bore our sicknesses." – Matthew 8:16-17

Jesus Christ took your place at the cross of Calvary. *His body was broken for you, so that you can be healed. His blood was shed for you, so that you can be forgiven*. He was wounded, bruised and scourged. *Isaiah 52:14* makes us to understand that He was disfigured beyond human recognition. *He physically felt in His body the agony of every sickness and disease ever known to man*. And why did He do it? It was for the sake of your own peace and well-being. *He took your weaknesses so you can become strong. He bore your diseases in order to carry them away.* He became sickness so that you can be healed (Isaiah 53:5) God is not the author of sickness and disease. *Jesus came so that you can have Zoe (the divine overcoming life)*. If you are a true believer, you now have *Zoe* within you. How can you take advantage of what Jesus has done? You do this by releasing and exercising your faith. *Your healing has been paid for; all you need do now is to claim what belongs to you by faith*. Command Satan to take his hands off your body. Command sickness to leave your body in the Name of Jesus. Confess that you are healed because of Jesus. *Proclaim that Himself took and bore it away!* (John 10:10).

Confession: *Satan has no right to put on me what God put on Jesus Christ. Himself took and bore it, in order to carry it away. Sin and sickness has passed from me to Calvary, and salvation and health have passed from Calvary to me.*

July 13
AUTHORITY NOW

Then the seventy returned with joy, saying, "Lord, even the demons are subject to us in Your name." And He said to them, "I saw Satan fall like lightning from heaven. Behold, I give you the authority to trample on serpents and scorpions, and over all the power of the enemy, and nothing shall by any means hurt you. – Luke 10:17-19

The Church is the body of Christ! This means that Christ functions in this world today through us. He is the head and we are His hands and feet. Jesus Christ has conferred His authority on the earth to His body (the Church). We have *authority now* to act in the place of Jesus Christ. Demons (evil spirits) cause a lot of trouble in this world. They are constantly behind the scene, manipulating men and situations to promote confusion, evil and ungodliness. As a true believer, you must know that the *Name of Jesus* belongs to you. This means that you have the *authority now*, to trample over all the power of the enemy. The demons are subject to you in the Name of Jesus, *and nothing shall by any means hurt you!* (Ephesians 1:20-23).

Many problems exist because we permit them. *How? Because we are not doing anything about them!* You are leaving it all up to God rather than using the authority that Christ Jesus has already delegated to you. *Take the Name of Jesus and break the power of the devil* in your life, in your home and in your family. *The devil should not do to you what he cannot do to Jesus!* (Matthew 28:18-20)

Prayer: *Dear Father, I thank You for giving Jesus Christ the Name above all names. Thank You because the Name of Jesus belongs to me today in the earth. I break the power of the devil over my life and home, in Jesus' Name. Amen.*

July 14
DEATH THROUGH SIN

Therefore, just as through one man sin entered the world, and death through sin, and thus death spread to all men, because all sinned. – Romans 5:12

When Adam sinned, he lost his spiritual dominion; with the resultant effect that darkness (spiritual death) started to reign in the earth (Romans 6:23). All of creation has been subjected to a bondage to decay and corruption (Romans 8:20-23). *This explains why life is broken.* For out of darkness comes decay, deformities, disease, defeat, destruction, disorder and death. Plants and animals (including the micro-organisms that cause sickness and disease) became wild in varying degrees. Man became a flesh-eater and his life-span shortened progressively from about 1,000 years (after *the Fall*) to about 100 years today. Notice that Satan could not rule on the earth until he got man to cooperate with him in disobedience and rebellion against God (John 8:42-44). So also, God cannot rule on the earth until He gets man to cooperate with him in *faith and obedience.* Through the disobedience of the first man: Adam, the earth and all its inhabitants became subject to the power of death and the bondage to decay. *Man lost his dominion to his adversary, the devil*, who then became the god (ruler) of this world system. *Every human is born with a fallen, sinful nature.* However, God has provided us *the free gift of righteousness and eternal life through Jesus Christ!* (Hebrews 11:6, 2 Corinthians 4:4, Romans 5:17-19).

Confession: *I have been delivered from the dominion of darkness. Jesus Christ is my head. I am a child of God and God is my very own Father. I reign in life through Jesus Christ. I reign over Sin, Sickness and Satan in Jesus' Name.*

July 15
UNION WITH GOD

… For you are the temple of the living God. As God has said: "I will dwell in them And walk among them. I will be their God, And they shall be My people." –2 Corinthians 6:16

The incarnation of the *eternal Word* as Jesus Christ is the first of many. He is the *second man* and the *last Adam* who is called to bring many sons unto glory. Those who believe and receive the eternal sacrifice of Jesus also experience this incarnation, for God comes to dwell inside their hearts (spirits) through His Holy Spirit. Can anything be more powerful than this? *The Greater One* now lives within you. If this is so, why are you still so weak and defeated? Is it because you don't recognise it, believe it, identify with it and proclaim it? (Philemon 1:6, Hebrews 10:23)

God's will cannot be done on the earth without the cooperation of man. The fact that you're born-again, a child of God, does not leave all the responsibility to God. God will do His part but you have to do yours. *Your part is not the supernatural; it's always a natural thing that you can do in obedience to the Word of God.* As a follower of Christ, all the promises of God in the Bible belong to you. You now have access by faith to the fullness of GRACE, which can be said to mean: 'God's Riches At Christ's Expense'. It's now your duty to believe the Word and appropriate it in your life on a daily basis. *The Word works if you go through the process!* You have peace with God and full access into His abundant GRACE (Romans 5:1-2).

Prayer: *Heavenly Father, I thank You for the vital union I have with You through Christ Jesus my Lord. I rejoice in my fellowship with You daily. Help me to stay conscious of Your presence within, and to live victoriously, in Jesus' Name.*

July 16
REJOICE IN THE LORD

Rejoice in the Lord always. Again I will say, rejoice!
– Philippians 4:4
**For the kingdom of God is not eating and drinking, but
righteousness and peace and joy in the Holy Spirit.**
– Romans 14:17

Happiness is a product of pleasant circumstances but *Joy is
a product of inner peace, which itself is the fruit of
righteousness*. Happiness is not always guaranteed in this
world which can be full of tests and trials. *However, Joy is a
divine product which is always available to you*. The Bible
talks about the *Joy of Salvation*. No matter what you are
currently going through, you can choose to rejoice in the
Lord. *Rejoicing in the Lord is an act of the will; it is a
decision to focus on the goodness and faithfulness of God.*
You are to rejoice because the Lord is good and His mercy
endures forever. He has promised to never leave you nor
forsake you. *You are to rejoice in the Lord always – no
matter the circumstances* (Isaiah 32:17, Hebrews 13:5-6).
How can you practise rejoicing in the Lord? *You 'rejoice in
the Lord' by praising Him!* An excellent way to praise is
singing. You rejoice in *righteousness*: the truth that you are
in right standing with God through Jesus Christ. *It is your
righteousness and trust in Him that gives you that sense of
inner peace and confidence in life*. You rejoice with psalms
and songs in the Spirit, thereby allowing the *Joy of the Holy
Spirit to bubble over* (Psalm 100, Ephesians 5:19).

Confession: *I praise You everlasting God, for You are good,
and Your mercies endure forever. You are faithful, holy, just
and true. You are El-Shaddai: 'the God who is more than
enough'. I rejoice in You always. Glory Hallelujah! Amen.*

July 17
HIDDEN WISDOM

But we speak the wisdom of God in a mystery, the hidden wisdom which God ordained before the ages for our glory, which none of the rulers of this age knew; for had they known, they would not have crucified the Lord of glory.
– 1 Corinthians 2:7-8

The Cross is Satan's defeat, for at the cross, the *Seed of the Woman* crushed the *head of the serpent* through His pure eternal sacrifice. The devil and his cohorts instigated both Jews and Gentiles to crucify Jesus. Satan thought he had finally got rid of the promised Seed and that Jesus Christ would remain under his prison in hell forever, for Jesus died as a man carrying the sins of other men. However, in Satan's delusion, he did not perceive that the shed blood of Jesus Christ is the eternal sacrifice that settles the debt of Sin and the punishment of Hell forever! (Genesis 3:15) Satan did not perceive that the justice of the Most High was now served through the cross, and that *the Heavenly Father* was able to raise the man *Jesus Christ* from 'death and hell' through the power of His *Holy Spirit*. The cross is the *hidden wisdom of God*. Just as *spiritual death* came to all from *a living tree of knowledge*, so also *spiritual life* is offered to all from *a dead tree of crucifixion* (Romans 5:17).

Having disarmed principalities and powers, He made a public spectacle of them, triumphing over them in it.
– Colossians 2:15

Prayer: *Thank You Father for Your hidden wisdom in sending Jesus Christ to die on the cross. Jesus has won for me a complete victory over spiritual death and eternal hell. I now reign in life through righteousness, in Jesus' Name.*

July 18
IGNORANCE IS FATAL

My people are destroyed for lack of knowledge.
Because you have rejected knowledge,
I also will reject you from being priest for Me;
Because you have forgotten the law of your God,
I also will forget your children.
— Hosea 4:6

Why do Christians suffer? Why doesn't God always favour His own people? In *Hosea 4:6*, God says that His people are *destroyed for lack of knowledge*. This means Christians are being defeated in life *because of their own ignorance*. It is not God's fault, for He has already provided all that you need in His written Word. *Your Bible is the most accurate representation of God that you have access to on this side of eternity*. What you do with it is up to you! *Don't say it's all up to God. No! It's all up to you!* Whatever you don't know in God's Word is what the devil is using to cheat and defeat you in life (Proverbs 23:23, 2 Timothy 2:15).

God is not a lawless God. He upholds all things by the Word of His power (Hebrews 1:3). Not all laws are equal. There are natural laws (e.g. gravity) and there are supernatural laws (e.g. faith). There are lower and higher laws. It is not just enough to understand the general principles of the Word. You have to dig deeper and study harder in order to access the deeper treasures of God. If you want to live victoriously, *you have to invest time to feed on God's word consistently and continuously*. And, yes, you can do it!

Confession: *The Word of God is true, alive and powerful. I refuse to be ignorant. I study and meditate on the Word, daily. I believe, confess and live by the Word, daily. The anointed Word is setting me free. Glory to God! Hallelujah!*

July 19
WATER AND BE WATERED

There is *one* who scatters, yet increases more;
And there is *one* who withholds more than is right,
But it *leads* to poverty. The generous soul will be made rich,
And he who waters will also be watered himself.
– Proverbs 11:25

Many Christians want God to bless them. Their prayer and song every day is 'bless me Lord, and bless me again'. The good news is that it is God's good pleasure to bless His children. *However, the real question is why does God bless you? It is so that you can be a blessing!* Having the material things of this world is not enough to make you blessed. You are only blessed as you become a blessing to others. That is why the Lord Jesus said: *It is more blessed to give than to receive*. A generous person is like a fountain of fresh water which waters the life of others to bring forth the most beautiful colours and fragrances (Acts 20:35).

Giving is the natural habit of every true believer. We give freely of our time, talents, money and resources. We have no qualms about paying our tithes and we rejoice in giving offerings to the Lord's work. *We are always sensitive to the needs of the church and the needs of others*. Are you in financial difficulty today? Could this be as a result of your withholding that which rightly belongs to the Lord? Why not repent and rededicate yourself to giving. As you do so, God will step in to your situation and show Himself strong on your behalf. *He is the Lord of the harvest* (Luke 6:38).

Prayer: *Almighty God, I thank You for all You have given me. There is nothing I have that I have not received. Help me to serve You faithfully with my time and money. Help to me to be faithful in giving generously in Jesus' Name. Amen*

July 20
HONOUR YOUR MARRIAGE

Marriage *is* honorable among all, and the bed undefiled; but fornicators and adulterers God will judge.
– Hebrews 13:4

The Bible says that *marriage is good and honourable in all!* Some people (such as Paul the Apostle) are called to abstain from marriage because of the special mission that God has given them. However, most people are called to marriage and should take advantage of it. *Marriage is a good thing, for two are better than one* (Ecclesiastes 4:9). If you are young and unmarried, you should save yourself for your future life partner. *Don't mess about with your body, for it belongs unto the Lord!* If you are a single, you should serve the Lord fervently, while trusting God for the right person to come along. The best way to wait is to get busy in God's work. Don't stay idle! *Flee from sexual immorality, for it a sin against your own body* (Romans 12:9-11).

If you are married, you need to pay attention to cultivating your marital garden daily, so that your flowers can keep producing the right colours and fragrances. *The devil does not like good things!* He will try his best to attack your marriage. It is up to you to refuse to give place to the devil. *Anything good in this life is worth protecting!* You do this by investing good words and actions into your marriage, daily! Don't get into the habit of destructive criticism and intolerance. *Why not invest more time into prayer for your spouse, and acts of selfless service?* (Ephesians 4:26-27)

Confession: I am a child of God and my life is governed by the Word of God. I refuse to be selfish and disobedient! I will honour and glorify God with my marriage. I will honour God with my body, words and actions daily, in Jesus' Name.

July 21
TRAIN THAT CHILD

**Train up a child in the way he should go,
And when he is old he will not depart from it.**
– Proverbs 22:6

The best legacy that you can give your children is to train them up in the way of the Lord (Ephesians 6:4). The Word of God is the Truth that sets men free. The Word is eternal seed which has life-producing power in itself. When you get your children *firmly rooted in the Word*, it will keep them going on the right path all through their lifetime, no matter the pressures of this world (Psalm 119:105,130).

Parents, teach your children to have a reverence for God and the things of God (Proverbs 9:10). The best way to do this is by your own personal example. If you would spend substantial time on worldly TV rather than in bible-study, prayer and fellowship, you are teaching your children that TV is more important than God. If you are mostly late to church or usually skip meetings, you are teaching them that church is not that important. If you are a poor giver, you are teaching them to be stingy. If you're cold, mean and unforgiving, they will pick it up. *Whatever you do daily and give priority to is what will dominate your children's worldview, even into adulthood!* You cannot afford to be careless, for children are impressionable. *You are to love them, discipline them and pray for them*. Don't just pray earthly things for them. Desire and pray always that the Word (Light) will dominate their hearts (Psalm 119:9-11).

Prayer: *Dear Heavenly Father, I thank You for the gift of life. I am responsible for my children. I will train and release them into their God-given destinies. Grant me wisdom to love, discipline and pray for them, in Jesus' Name. Amen.*

July 22
PURIFIED BY FIRE

Now if anyone builds on this foundation with gold, silver, precious stones, wood, hay, straw, each one's work will become clear; for the Day will declare it, because it will be revealed by fire; and the fire will test each one's work, of what sort it is. If anyone's work which he has built on it endures, he will receive a reward. If anyone's work is burned, he will suffer loss; but he himself will be saved, yet so as through fire.
– 1 Corinthians 3:12-15

As a true believer in Christ, you need to be aware that you are building into the kingdom every day of your life. <u>Be careful how you build!</u> *Will you appear before your Lord and master empty-handed, with nothing to show for your lifetime on the earth?* Start living for Him! The good works that will survive the judgement seat are those that are done in *faith and obedience* to the Lord. *All works based on selfish motives and false doctrines will be consumed by fire*, for Christ must present the church to Himself as a glorious church. Don't lose your rewards! Don't lose your crowns! Start building your *eternal inheritance* with good quality material: *faith, hope and love* (1 Corinthians 13:13).

Only true believers shall appear at *the judgement seat of Christ* (2 Corinthians 5:10). False believers and unbelievers will appear at *the great white throne judgement* to receive sentencing unto the eternal lake of fire (Revelation 20:11-15). *The purpose of the judgement seat is for purification and rewards. Don't lose your rewards!* (Ephesians 5:26-27).

Confession: *I am created in Christ Jesus unto good works. I refuse to live selfishly. I will walk by faith. I will walk in love. I will preach the gospel. I will pay my tithes. I will serve in the church. I will support the man of God. I will be faithful.*

July 23
HOLD FAST YOUR CONFESSION

Therefore, holy brethren, partakers of the heavenly calling, consider the Apostle and High Priest of our confession, Christ Jesus. – Hebrews 3:1
Seeing then that we have a great High Priest who has passed through the heavens, Jesus the Son of God, let us hold fast *our* confession. – Hebrews 4:14

Jesus Christ is the High Priest of our confession! This means that He watches over what we say in agreement with His Word, in order to perform it. The radical idea in this verse is that our *High Priest* cannot function effectively on our behalf without our own confession. This includes both the *confession of our sins* according to *1 John 1:9* and the *confession of our faith* according to *Hebrews 10:23*. What have you been saying about what you're believing for? Don't talk foolishly! *What you say with your mouth must agree with what you're believing for in your heart.*

The main reason why the faith of many is not working is the disconnect between their hearts and mouths. They pray and believe for something, yet they run their mouths wild in contradiction to what they are believing for. Some people make a habit of speaking negative all the time. *No!* When you truly believe, you are to <u>hold fast</u> to your confession of faith. How do you 'hold fast'? *You say it and keep saying it, irrespectively of contrary evidence.* You hold fast with the tenacity of a bull dog: no backing off, until you get your desired result (Hebrews 10:35-39).

Prayer: *Almighty and Everlasting God, I thank You because Thy Word is Truth. Facts change but truth remains. I will study and meditate upon Your Word. I will believe and hold fast to my confession of Your Word, in Jesus' Name. Amen.*

July 24
WISDOM AND FAVOUR

And Jesus increased in wisdom and stature, and in favor with God and men. – Luke 2:52

Wisdom and Favour will help you become truly successful in the sight of God and men. Your journey of success starts with divine Wisdom, which comes from above. *You must set your heart on wisdom and refuse to live foolishly!* Wisdom is not the same thing as smartness: you can be smart and yet foolish. *Wisdom starts from putting God (the source of wisdom) first*. Put Him in the place of highest priority in your life. You cannot say that you love God and yet treat the things of God (church worship service, home fellowship, prayer meeting etc.) nonchalantly. *Treating the things of God shabbily is foolishness!* That is why Jesus, even at 12 years old, told His parents that He must be about His Father's business. No wonder, He increased in wisdom, stature and favour (Luke 2:48-52, Proverbs 9:10).
Favour is the natural by-product of walking in Wisdom. As you walk in obedience to the Word and Spirit, the favour of God begins to dominate your life. God has the power to bring you into favour with men (Proverbs 16:7). Rather than being termed forsaken, you will be called *Hephzibah, because the Lord delights in you* (Isaiah 62:4). Your active connection with God opens the door for uncommon favour with men, just as God brought Joseph into favour with the Pharaoh of Egypt. You will need favour in your life. *One day of favour is worth a thousand days of hard labour!*

Confession: *Divine Wisdom is from above, giving me discernment and direction in life. I refuse to be foolish! I embrace obedience to the Word. I stay in active connection with God and I walk in His divine favour, in Jesus' Name.*

July 25
WHATEVER YOU PERMIT

And I will give you the keys of the kingdom of heaven, and whatever you bind on earth will be bound in heaven, and whatever you loose on earth will be loosed in heaven.
– Matthew 16:19

In *Matthew 16:13-20*, after Peter had affirmed Jesus as the Christ (the anointed one, the Messiah of mankind), the Son of the living God, Jesus proclaimed that He will build His Church and the gates of Hell shall not prevail against it. *Why will the gates of hell not prevail against the church?* It is because Jesus has won the victory over the devil through His *death, burial and resurrection*. He defeated the devil soundly, and obtained the keys of death and hell from him. Those same keys have been handed over to us because we are the body of Christ (Colossians 2:15, Revelation 1:18).

What keys does the Church have? We have the powerful Name of Jesus, the Name above all names (Philippians 2:9-11). In the original language, "whatever you bind on earth" refers to: *whatever you permit on earth* and "whatever you loose on earth" refers to: *whatever you refuse on earth*. This is not referring to binding the devil. *No!* It refers to taking authority over the forces of darkness and nature. You are to take the Name of Jesus and break the power of the devil over your life, home and family. *We've permitted a lot of things because we haven't exercised our authority*. You can choose to refuse certain events from dominating your life or community. *Take a firm stand by faith!*

Prayer: *Almighty God, I thank You for the authority I have in the Name of Jesus. I refuse to allow Satan to dominate me in any area of my life. Thank You, for Heaven backs me up whenever I take a firm stand by faith, in Jesus' Name.*

July 26
PREDESTINED TO BECOME

For whom He foreknew, He also predestined *to be* conformed to the image of His Son, that He might be the firstborn among many brethren. – Romans 8:29

Have you ever thought about what is the main purpose of your Christian journey on the earth? The answer is: '*to become like Jesus*'. Do you know that the word 'Christian' means Christ-like? The advent of Jesus into the world is not an afterthought of God. It was an original plan made by God, having foreseen the fall of Adam at the Garden of Eden. *God's eternal plan is to redeem men into <u>His Eternal Family</u> by New Birth*. In this regard, Jesus Christ is the *Last Adam* (Only two men in history were a direct creation of God: Adam and Jesus Christ). Note that Jesus Christ was incarnated, for He always existed (1 Corinthians 15:45-49). Adam sinned before He could reproduce spiritual life. However, Jesus Christ lived without Sin, paid its price by His crucifixion, and broke its power by His resurrection. *Therefore, only Jesus can give eternal life to men by New Birth*. In this regard, He is the *Firstborn* from the dead and the *Second Man* with new spiritual life. He is the firstborn because you also have been made a son of God through faith in Jesus. God's purpose in doing this is so that you may in all things grow up to become like Him. *Study the lifestyle of Jesus in the Gospels*. God's plan for you is to become like Him. *You are to think, speak and act like Jesus, for you now belong to Jesus, totally!* (Ephesians 4:13-16)

Confession: *I am a new creation in Christ. Divine life flows within me. I feed my spirit with the Word. I renew my mind with the Word. I subject my body to the supremacy of my spirit. I am becoming conformed to the image of the Son.*

July 27
LIVING FOR THE GOSPEL

So Jesus answered and said, "Assuredly, I say to you, there is no one who has left house or brothers or sisters or father or mother or wife or children or lands, for My sake and the gospel's, who shall not receive a hundredfold now in this time ..., with persecutions—and in the age to come, eternal life.
— Mark 10:29-30

The steering wheel of Christian service is the Great Commission (Mark 16:14-18). God's plan in *history* is the plan of *redemption*. Therefore, the redemption of souls into the kingdom of Heaven is at the heart of our service to the Lord. All our abilities, gifts, trainings and resources in life are useless if they don't *ultimately contribute* to the plan of redemption. Now is the time to *live life to the fullest*, by using all that you are and all that you have to serve the Lord faithfully, so that the kingdom of God on the earth can grow and flourish (2 Corinthians 5:18-19).

Some people think that if they commit to serving God, they will miss out on the good things of life. They are very keen on enjoying comfort and acceptance. *They are afraid of rejection and persecution*. However, they forget that every good and perfect gift comes from above (James 1:17). Jesus Himself has promised to reward His faithful servants abundantly <u>in this life</u>. *Don't waste your life! Anything you do in this life that doesn't ultimately contribute to God's purpose (worship) and plan (redemption) is a waste of time and will not count in eternity* (1 Corinthians 3:11-15).

Prayer: *Dear Father in Heaven, I rededicate myself to You. Help me to serve You faithfully with everything I have. Grant me wisdom and boldness to preach the good news of salvation to the world around me, in Jesus' Name. Amen.*

July 28
THE PATH OF LIFE

You will show me the path of life;
In Your presence *is* fullness of joy;
At Your right hand *are* pleasures forevermore.
— Psalm 16:11

In *John 1:4*, the Bible says that: *In Him was life, and the life was the light of men*. This life refers to *Zoe: the divine overcoming life of God*. <u>Zoe is the light of men</u>. Those who do not have Zoe in them have no light. They're still walking in the darkness of this world and need to be saved. *Where is the Path of Life*? *In His Presence!* The pathway of Zoe is to spend time exclusively in the presence of the Most High, daily. You enter into his gates with thanksgiving and come into His courts with praise. The divine life that has been deposited into your inner man when you got born-again becomes *increasingly activated* as you spend quality time in communion with the Holy Trinity (Father, Son and Holy Spirit). You are to live before and within his presence daily. *Live with a conscious awareness of His presence, daily!*

Don't ever forget that you are in *personal relationship* with God! *Your quiet time* with God daily is a time spent with *full concentration* on God: in Bible study, meditation, praise, prayer and listening. When you spend time *In His Presence*, you will experience a continuous supply of inner peace, which will overflow into the fullness of Joy. *Spending time in exclusive personal focus on the Lord daily is a vital act of abiding in Christ* (John 15:4, Psalm 84).

Confession: *I am a child of God. He is my very own Father and I am His very own child. I am in personal relationship with Him. Therefore I delight myself in Him. I delight in spending a personal quiet time In His Presence, daily!*

July 29
PERSECUTED FOR RIGHTEOUSNESS

Yes, and all who desire to live godly in Christ Jesus will suffer persecution. But evil men and impostors will grow worse and worse, deceiving and being deceived.
– 2 Timothy 3:12-13

As true believers, we must remember that although we are in this world, we are not of this world (John 17:16). The Bible says that *Satan is the god of this world system*. He took over dominion when Adam fell. This present world is in darkness. *God is not ruling the world currently, but He will one day*. Right now, God's will is being carried out only in the lives of those who surrender to Him. *The world loves 'fancy, pleasure and fun' but it doesn't love righteousness*. Therefore, the world will always persecute those who stand up for the infallible Word of God and determine to live a godly life (2 Corinthians 4:4, 1 John 5:19, John 12:46). If you are a true believer, you can expect persecution from unbelievers and false believers. *I'm talking about being persecuted for righteousness, <u>not wrong-doing</u>!* People will take offence when you honour the Name of Jesus, preach the gospel or invite them to church. They will take offence when you refuse to lie, curse, drink, cheat or compromise divine truths. *Never allow yourself to become discouraged. Just maintain your fellowship with God and true believers.* <u>God will surely reward you</u>! Satan's running a lot of things, but he's not running us. *We are to dominate him and break his power in the Name of Jesus* (Matthew 5:10-12).

Prayer: *Almighty God, I thank You for Your goodness and faithfulness. Thank You for the privilege to live and stand for righteousness. Grant me grace to endure persecution, knowing that my reward in Christ is great, in Jesus' Name.*

July 30
NOT FORSAKEN

... For He Himself has said, "I will never leave you nor forsake you." So we may boldly say: "The Lord *is* my helper; I will not fear. What can man do to me?" – Hebrews 13:5-6

Many times, the reason why we are worried and fearful is because we are more conscious of man and nature, than we are of God. Although Goliath was a mighty giant and an experienced warrior, teenager *David resized him using the measuring instrument of Heaven*. He said "who is this uncircumcised Philistine, that he should defy the armies of the living God?" (1 Samuel 17:26). Don't pray to God not to forsake you. Why? *He has already promised in His Word that He will never leave you nor forsake you*. That is a more sure word of prophecy that cannot fail (Psalm 119:89).

Whether the sun is shining or the rain is falling, He is with you and He's got your back. How do you activate this promise in the times of trial and hardship? You are to <u>boldly say</u>: *"The Lord is my helper; I will not fear. What can man do to me?"* You are to speak boldly because the righteous are as bold as a lion, according to *Proverbs 28:1*. You say that God is your helper because *He is your very present help in trouble*, according to *Psalm 46:1*. You refuse to fear because fear opens the door to oppression, accordingly to *Isaiah 54:14*. You say 'what can man do to me' because you know that the fear of man brings a snare, according to *Proverbs 29:25*. As you declare your trust in God, He will surely make a way for you (Isaiah 43:19).

Confession: I'm a child of El-Shaddai: The God who is more than enough. I refuse to be dominated by worry and fear! God is with me. He will not forsake me. I boldly say that the Lord is my helper, I will not fear. What can man do to me?

July 31
NOT IN VAIN

Therefore, my beloved brethren, be steadfast, immovable, always abounding in the work of the Lord, knowing that your labor is not in vain in the Lord. – 1 Corinthians 15:58

Jesus Christ is coming back, not as a gentle Saviour but as an all-conquering King. He will judge the nations and He will reward every single person according to their *work of Faith, labour of Love and patience of Hope*. We must be encouraged to put in our very best for our Lord in this life. Don't allow the selfishness and nonchalant behaviour of others to discourage you. Don't compare yourself with them, for they are yet dominated by spiritual blindness. *It's your own race that you are running, not theirs at all.* Your personal obedience is the seed for their own revival. *Everyone will stand before Jesus Christ on judgement day as an individual.* Therefore, run your race in such a way as to obtain the prize (1 Corinthians 9:24, Philippians 3:14). There is only one way to live without regrets: walk in love. *Make the most of every opportunity to please God and bless lives every day.* There is no room for laziness and procrastination where it pertains to kingdom business. *Seek first the kingdom of God each day!* Today is the opportunity you have to move forward. What you do today is your seed for tomorrow's harvest. *Don't ever forget that God is a rewarder of those who diligently seek Him. Therefore, you can rest assured in Him that your labour of love will never be in vain* (Hebrews 11:6).

Prayer: *Father God, thank You for the opportunity I have to invest in Your kingdom. I choose to seek first Your kingdom. I refuse to live selfishly. I receive Grace to live by faith, walk in love, preach, pray, give and serve, in Jesus' Name. Amen.*

August 1
HE HEARS US

Now this is the confidence that we have in Him, that if we ask anything according to His will, He hears us. And if we know that He hears us, whatever we ask, we know that we have the petitions that we have asked of Him. – 1 John 5:14-15

God's Word is God's will. Therein we find everything that God has willed to His children. The depth of your prayer life cannot go beyond your knowledge of God's Word. *You will become more effective in prayer as you become more established in God's Word*. You cannot become established in God's Word without giving it high priority in your daily routine. This is why those who do not study the Word regularly will continue to pray like spiritual babies. *As you become more established in the Word, you will increase in your sensitivity to God's voice and God's will*. Your faith will begin to grow, and you will approach your Heavenly Father in prayer with increased confidence (Hebrews 11:6).

In *John 11:41-42*, when Jesus wanted to raise Lazarus from the dead, He thanked *the Father* for having heard Him, and also declared 'I know that You always hear Me'. *If you know that the Father hears you, He will hear you!* If you know that the Father hears you, whatever you ask, then you can have confidence to receive what you have asked of Him. *How can you receive from God when you have no confidence in Him?* Our Lord Jesus already told us that whatever we ask the Father in His Name, He will give it to us. *You are to approach God by His Word* (Hebrews 4:16).

Prayer: *Thank You Father for loving me with an everlasting love. Thank You because You are my very own Father, and You hear me when I pray. I commit myself to be full of Your Word. I pray in line with Your Word always, in Jesus' Name.*

August 2
BENEFITS OF REDEMPTION

Christ has redeemed us from the curse of the law, having become a curse for us (for it is written, "Cursed is everyone who hangs on a tree"), that the blessing of Abraham might come upon the Gentiles in Christ Jesus, that we might receive the promise of the Spirit through faith. – Galatians 3:13-14

The *mathematical formula* for victorious living is called: *Substitution*. This is *accessed through faith*. The <u>eternal sacrifice of Jesus Christ</u> is the platform for redemption and the basis for supernatural victory in all circumstances. This is because the sacrifice of Jesus restores the believing man into a legal union with God, such that the dominion lost in Adam is now regained in Christ. This is redemption at work! The eternal sacrifice of Jesus Christ involves a *seven-fold divine exchange* as follows:

He was punished that we might be forgiven.
He was wounded that we might be healed.
He died our death that we might share His Life.
He endured the curse
that we might enjoy the blessing.
He endured our poverty
that we might share His abundance.
He endured our shame
that we might share His glory.
He endured our rejection
that we might share His acceptance.
Take advantage of divine substitution through faith today!

Confession: *Christ has redeemed me from the curse by becoming a curse for me. He took my place. I am redeemed from spiritual death, sickness, disease, poverty and satanic oppression. I live in the fullness of blessing, in Jesus' Name.*

August 3
WINNING BY FAITH

For with the heart one believes unto righteousness, and with the mouth confession is made unto salvation.
– Romans 10:10

Many Christians may wonder why they are not winning. Well now, if all you ever gave attention to was secular entertainment, secular refreshment, secular training and secular pursuits, how could you ever achieve anything spiritual or supernatural? *You've got to give quality attention to spiritual food (the Word) and to spiritual drink (the Spirit).* You've got to give quality attention to <u>faith and obedience</u>. Give attention to a personal quiet time with God daily, walking in love, and genuine fellowship with true believers. *Faith comes by hearing!* (Romans 10:17).

I cannot overemphasize the point that you cannot afford to spend more time on secular media, as compared to godly media. *Whatever you are consuming daily is what will dominate your mind.* You cannot afford to be addicted to worldly movies, for they are full of <u>language, violence and nudity</u>. These things will make you struggle. *Fill your life with the Word!* You have a responsibility to believe and appropriate the Word for yourself. If you have faith as small as a mustard seed, you will SAY and SPEAK to your mountain (Matthew 17:20). If you are not speaking your faith, it remains dormant and ineffective, for death and life are in the power of the tongue (Proverbs 18:21*). You are to speak life, and not death.* What have you been saying?

Prayer: *Dear Father, thank You for Your holy written Word which reveals Your will to me. Help me to keep away from worldly influence. Help me to fill my life with Your Word, daily. I choose to live and win by faith, in Jesus' Name.*

August 4
SET THE LORD

I have set the Lord always before me;
Because *He is* at my right hand I shall not be moved.
– Psalm 16:8

Psalm 125:1 makes us to understand that those who trust in the Lord cannot be shaken. They are like Mount Zion which abides forever! When I read this, the question that goes through my mind is: what does it mean to 'trust in the Lord'. *I do not like to be shaken by any event. Do you?* Obviously, trusting in the Lord refers to 'believing or having faith in God'. However, there is much more involved. *Trusting includes being focused, firm, and resolute*. When you focus on the Lord, stand firmly on His Word, and make a resolute decision not to let go, nothing else in this world can move you. That is why the Psalmist says: I have set the Lord always before me. *In other words, I have set my gaze and hope firmly on the Lord* (Psalm 34:5, Hebrews 10:23).

How do you set your gaze firmly on the Lord? You do this by putting His Word in the place of <u>highest priority</u> in your life. You settle it once and for all that His Word is the <u>final authority</u> in your life. You spend time meditating on the Word. You spend time praying to your Heavenly Father. You spend time in regular fellowship with true believers. *As you set the Lord always before you, His presence will begin to dominate your life.* You will become confident that He is at your right hand. Therefore, you begin to *speak to move* circumstances, rather than them moving you.

Confession: *I have set the Lord always before me. His Word is the final authority in my life. I spend quality time meditating and praying. I spend time in regular fellowship with true believers. I shall not be moved, in Jesus' Name.*

August 5
LOVE YOUR ENEMIES

But I say to you, love your enemies, bless those who curse you, do good to those who hate you, and pray for those who spitefully use you and persecute you, that you may be sons of your Father in heaven; for He makes His sun rise on the evil and on the good, and sends rain on the just and on the unjust. – Matthew 5:44-45

It is very natural to love your friend and hate your enemy. Who is your enemy? Someone who dislikes you and wishes to do you harm. How then can Jesus tell us to love our enemies, bless those who curse us, do good to those who hate us and pray for those who treat us badly? *This seems to be an extreme command which is not possible to obey with our natural human love*. However, that is where the God-kind of love comes in. Only a *selfless sacrificial and overflowing* love can obey this golden commandment of Jesus Christ. *The good news is that you already have God's nature of love within you, as a true believer in Christ.* You are to let this love blossom and dominate you completely. You walk in love by faith! (Romans 5:5, Hebrews 10:38).
Has someone hurt you beyond repair? Don't hold on too tightly! Forgive and release them to God. The Lord says that *'vengeance is mine'*. He can surely sort them out! Always seek to bless people, for God sends His rain on the just and the unjust. *Your warfare is more spiritual than physical. Use the spiritual weapons of faith, hope and love to overcome evil with good* (Romans 12:19-21).

Prayer: *Almighty God, my fervent desire is to know and love You more. You are gracious and compassionate, slow to anger and rich in love. As I've received Your love freely, help me to give it out freely to others, in Jesus' Name.*

August 6
GOD IS JUST

For I proclaim the name of the Lord: Ascribe greatness to our God. *He is* the Rock, His work *is* perfect; For all His ways *are* justice, A God of truth and without injustice; Righteous and upright *is* He. – Deuteronomy 32:3-4

The Most High is Just and He is eternally committed to justice. He is unchangeable, unshakeable and unstoppable. *No human being is fully qualified to define what is fair, for we are all influenced by selfish tendencies from time to time.* However, God is righteous and holy. He is sinless and stainless. He knows the hearts of men, and weighs their actions and intentions according to His perfect moral standard. God is faithful and true to His Word. He cannot condone unrighteousness! (1 Samuel 2:3, James 1:17)

You cannot hide (your sin) from God, for He knows about everything. The judgements of God during our life on earth are temporal, an extension of His mercy, in order to bring us to repentance and blessing. The judgements of God when we pass on from this life are final and eternal. Every man will be judged according to how they lived on earth with respect to the purpose of God. Their eternal place is determined by their faith in response to God's Love and their eternal state is determined by their works in response to God's Word. *The justice of God glorifies His holiness and the glory of God is the greatest goal of all existence.* Therefore, throughout all of eternity, God must continuously be glorified (Acts 17:31, Revelations 20:15).

Confession: *I worship and serve the only true and living God. He is righteous, faithful and just. He is a rewarder of those who diligently seek Him. He will judge the wicked and unbelieving. He will judge all unrighteousness. Hallelujah!*

August 7
HE WILL TEACH YOU

But the Helper, the Holy Spirit, whom the Father will send in My name, He will teach you all things, and bring to your remembrance all things that I said to you. – John 14:26

As a true believer in Christ, do you know that you have a *Divine Teacher* within you? He is the Holy Spirit – the third person of the Holy Trinity. *He lives within you to lead you into all truth*. Jesus said that the Holy Spirit will teach and remind us everything that He has said. This means that the Spirit will illuminate the Word of God (the Bible) to us. He will reveal to us the divine truths of the Word as we spend time in meditation and fellowship daily. *The Holy Spirit <u>cannot</u> lead you contrary to the Bible. He will always and only teach you in line with the Word*. Moreover, He will bring important Bible truths (which you already studied) to your remembrance in your times of need (John 14:16-17).
Learn to rely on the Holy Spirit. Talk to Him regularly. Ask for His help often. He is your Divine Helper and Teacher. No one fancies being ignored! Don't live a self-centred life that habitually ignores the Holy Spirit, for when you ignore Him, you are grieving Him. He is a sweet and gentle Spirit who will not force Himself over you. He acts gently to stimulate your spirit and you must be sensitive to yield and respond to Him. *No believer can live victoriously in this world without embracing the ministry of the Holy Spirit*. That is why He is here to abide with you forever. He is your seal unto the day of redemption (Ephesians 4:30).

Prayer: *Heavenly Father, I thank You for the ministry of Your Holy Spirit in my life today. Thank You for the well of living water that dwells inside me. Help me to stay in active continuous fellowship with the Holy Spirit, in Jesus' Name.*

August 8
BUILD UP SPIRITUALLY

But you, beloved, building yourselves up on your most holy faith, praying in the Holy Spirit, keep yourselves in the love of God, looking for the mercy of our Lord Jesus Christ unto eternal life. – Jude 1:20-21

There may be times when you're feeling low or upset; or times when your heart is troubled. Some people respond to these situations by getting irritable, binging on food or unwinding with secular entertainment. However, the best way to respond to the burdens of life is to edify yourself (build yourself up spiritually) by praying in the Holy Ghost. Praying in tongues extensively helps to stimulate your faith and keep you in love; *it lifts you up to a heightened level of spiritual sensitivity and inspiration* (Ephesians 6:18).

When any true believer is baptised (filled) with the Holy Spirit, they receive the confirming sign of *a spiritual overflow, that is: the gift of tongues. Tongues are a prayer and prophecy language*; a means by which the Holy Spirit helps us in our weaknesses (Romans 8:26-27). Praying in the Spirit is an act of faith: you yield your tongue to the Holy Spirit, and you speak out divine utterances (by faith) from your innermost being. *Don't be afraid to start off mechanically!* As you persist by faith, *rivers of living water* will flow forth from your inner man (John 7:38-39). Praying in tongues enables you to pray perfectly for yourself and others. *When you build up yourself by praying in tongues extensively, your inner peace and joy will be renewed.*

Confession: *The Spirit of the living God dwells within me. I believe I receive the fullness of the Spirit. I build myself up in faith by praying in tongues regularly. Through tongues, I release the supernatural upon my world. Hallelujah! Amen.*

August 9
SET YOUR MIND

If then you were raised with Christ, seek those things which are above, where Christ is, sitting at the right hand of God. Set your mind on things above, not on things on the earth.
– Colossians 3:1-2

Some Christians live as if their dwelling place (comfort, achievement and possessions) on earth is more important than their dwelling place in Heaven. Such people are afraid that the world will end suddenly, without their enjoying all that it has to offer. *Is Heaven really as glorious as the Bible says?* If so, why are you not investing into your Heavenly inheritance? *Why are you laying up your treasure on earth, where moth and rust can destroy?* (Matthew 6:19-21)

Don't you know that the world is passing away? (1 John 2:17). If you have been raised with Christ, then you should seek first the kingdom of God. *Let the things of God be your topmost priority in life*. This includes serving God in the church, giving, and preaching the gospel. *Set your mind on things above!* If you focus your thoughts on worldly things, you will become worldly. If you focus your thoughts on godly things, you will become godly. Your dominant thoughts should be about pleasing God and seeing His kingdom advance on the earth. *Your attitude to the things of God matters a lot!* Don't go late to church and don't skip meetings habitually. God is seeking for *true worshippers* (John 4:23-24): those who will worship Him in spirit (with all their heart) and in truth (without hypocrisy).

Prayer: *Almighty and Everlasting God, You deserve all the glory, honour and praise. I want my life to be focussed on pleasing You. I want to know You intimately, love You deeply and serve You faithfully, in Jesus' Name.* Amen.

August 10
DIALOGUE TO RESOLVE

Moreover if your brother sins against you, go and tell him his fault between you and him alone. If he hears you, you have gained your brother. But if he will not hear, take with you one or two more, that 'by the mouth of two or three witnesses every word may be established.' – Matthew 18:15-16

Unforgiveness and bitterness are cankerworms that will rob you of God's best for your life. People will always offend you: it is a fundamental result of human weakness. However, not everyone who offends you realise what they have done as you see it. Many are just being themselves, never mind the selfishness involved. *If your brother offends you, go and tell him his fault rather than making room for bitterness.* Speak the truth in love. Use dialogue rather than destructive criticism. *Mind your language!* Explain how you have been offended and listen to the person's explanation. Tell him his fault between you and him alone; don't jump into slander and malice. *Enter into dialogue with the mindset of conflict resolution. Don't aim to win; rather aim to resolve* (Ephesians 4:15, Romans 12:18).

Forgiving those who have offended you is not an option; it is the only way forward. Therefore, make every necessary effort to reconcile those who have offended you. However, the outcome is not always positive. Some will refuse to admit their faults, even after involving others to resolve the conflict. In these circumstances, your conscience will be clear. *You just keep walking in love* (Hebrews 12:14-15).

Confession: *I am a child of God. His love dwells within my heart. There is no room for unforgiveness and bitterness in me. I release all those who have offended me. I forgive them because of Jesus. I am free from offences. Hallelujah!*

August 11
TAKE CORRECTION

**Whoever loves instruction loves knowledge,
But he who hates correction *is* stupid.**
– Proverbs 12:1

You cannot improve in any aspect of life without discipline and training. In like manner, you cannot grow spiritually without embracing instruction and taking correction from your God-appointed leaders. Don't think that you have outgrown correction because you are an adult. No! *The journey to spiritual maturity (true maturity) is a life-long process*. Your ultimate goal is <u>to become</u> conformed to the image of the Son. *Beware of pride and stubbornness! Beware of self-righteousness* (Proverbs 29:1, Romans 8:29) Some people detest being corrected or rebuked. They so much believe in their right to speak and act as they like. However, this type of behaviour is not fitting for a child of God. It is symptomatic of inward pride, and a major hindrance to spiritual progress. *God resists the proud but give more grace to the humble* (James 4:6). We all have to re-assess our priorities in life from time to time. *What are you seeking to become? Does God have any place in your goals and ambitions? Does Jesus have the very first place in your life?* If so, your primary purpose in life will be <u>to please the lord</u>. This involves honouring the Church of God and the man of God. *Yes indeed, God loves you. However, He corrects those He loves*. He does this so that you can grow and be a partaker of His holiness (Hebrews 12:5-11).

Prayer: *Almighty and Everlasting God, I rededicate myself to You: spirit, soul and body. I embrace an attitude of 'humility and obedience'. Help me to be teachable. Help me to be submissive to godly authority, in Jesus' Name. Amen.*

August 12
AUTHORITY OVER DISEASE

Then He called His twelve disciples together and gave them power and authority over all demons, and to cure diseases. He sent them to preach the kingdom of God and to heal the sick.
— Luke 9:1-2

Are you a true disciple of the Lord Jesus? If so, you have authority over all demons and diseases. You have authority in the Name of Jesus to heal the sick, cleanse the lepers, raise the dead and cast out evil spirits. This authority has been delegated to you by Jesus Christ when He rose up from the dead, having defeated Sin, Satan, Death and Hell. *You are a member of the body of Christ and He functions through you in this world* (Matthew 10:8, Mark 16:17-18).
Where does sickness and disease come from? There is no disease up in Heaven! *Sickness is the foul offspring of its father: Satan and its mother: Sin.* Christ is our head and we are the members of His body. *Can sickness and disease dominate Jesus?   Well, if it can't dominate the head, it has no right to dominate the body*. Satan does not have any authority to rule over you. The messengers of Satan (sin, sickness and poverty) should not rule over you. You need to believe and confess it (Colossians 1:18, Ephesians 1:22).
How do you exercise your spiritual authority over disease?
Command it to leave your body in the Name of Jesus. Command infection, aches and pains to leave! Release the prayer of faith, according to *James 5:15* and *Mark 11:24*. Refuse sickness and disease from dominating you!

Confession: *Jesus Christ became a curse, so I can enjoy the blessing. He became sickness, so I can enjoy health. I walk in divine health and healing. I refuse to be sick! I command you sickness and disease to leave my body, in Jesus' Name.*

August 13
THE BLOOD SPEAKS

But you have come to Mount Zion and to the city of the living God, the heavenly Jerusalem, to an innumerable company of angels, to the general assembly and church of the firstborn *who are* registered in heaven, to God the Judge of all, to the spirits of just men made perfect, to Jesus the Mediator of the new covenant, and to the blood of sprinkling that speaks better things than *that of* Abel. – Hebrews 12:22-24

The sacrificial shedding of pure animal blood represents atonement: one life given for another. This is why the first blood sacrifice took place in the Garden of Eden, after the fall of Adam and Eve. God covered their sin and nakedness with animal blood and skin. However, the blood of *pure unblemished* animals can only atone for sins temporarily; it cannot take away the Sin problem. *Only a supernatural lamb would be sufficient.* The precious blood of Jesus, shed at the cross of Calvary, is the basis for the redemption of all mankind (Genesis 3:21, Hebrews 9:22, 1 Peter 1:19-20). *The blood speaks!* In *Genesis 4*, we read that when Cain killed his brother Abel due to anger and jealousy, the blood of Abel cried out to the Lord from the ground. The blood cried for vengeance and Cain became accursed. *However, the blood of Jesus speaks better things than that of Abel*. It speaks forgiveness and righteousness. *It speaks Salvation, Healing and Deliverance*. It speaks victory over the devil and all powers of darkness. *There is power mighty in the blood of Jesus Christ!* (Hebrews 9:13-14, Revelation 12:11).

Prayer: *Dear Father, I thank You for the precious blood of Jesus Christ. There is power mighty in the blood of Jesus Christ. It speaks for me! I cover myself, my family, all that I am, and all that I have, with the precious blood of Jesus.*

August 14
FREEDOM AND BONDAGE

Therefore do not let sin reign in your mortal body, that you should obey it in its lusts. And do not present your members *as* instruments of unrighteousness to sin, but present yourselves to God as being alive from the dead, and your members *as* instruments of righteousness to God. – Romans 6:12-13

Freedom is defined as the power or right to act, speak, or think as one wants. However, true freedom can only be guaranteed by order. Imagine what it will be like for several cars to drive on the highway without any traffic rules. Wouldn't that be disaster? *Freedom can only be guaranteed by appropriate moral boundaries; otherwise it will lead to chaos.* This is why *free* societies must be governed by the rule of law. Limitless freedom always leads to bondage. *God is the limitless Limit that guarantees true freedom*. This is because He is the most worthy person to define the moral standard, since He is the Most High who is *Just* and possesses *Infinite Wisdom* (Romans 8:2).

It was *pride* that led to the Fall of Satan and it can be rightly said that *pride is the greatest sin ever, for it leads to deliberate rebellion against the Most High*. God resists the proud but gives grace to the humble (James 4:6). So we see that the only way for man to experience true freedom is to 'trust and obey' God. However, a life of obedience cannot be achieved without an attitude of humility. *Obedience and humility go together*. *Obedience is the greatest human responsibility* (Isaiah 2:12, Proverbs 3:5-6).

Confession: *I refuse to live in bondage to Sin, Sickness or Satan. The law of Life (Light and Love) has set me free from the law of sin and death. I refuse to be proud and stubborn. I embrace humility and obedience in Jesus' Name. Amen.*

August 15
REIGNING IN LIFE

For if by the one man's offense death reigned through the one, much more those who receive abundance of grace and of the gift of righteousness will reign in life through the One, Jesus Christ. – Romans 5:17

The greatest asset that God has given to every person is free will: the ability to make choices. Your will emanates from your spirit and is enacted in your soul. It is your own responsibility to repent of your sins and believe the gospel of Jesus Christ. It is your own responsibility to reign in life. *It is not all up to God. It is all up to you!* As a true believer in Jesus Christ, you have received abundance of grace through Christ and a right standing with God through Christ (i.e. the same standing of Christ) so that you can reign as a king in your domain in this life through Christ. What are you to reign over? Sin, sickness, disease, poverty, oppression, depression, demons, and every other form of spiritual darkness. Does *Romans 5:17* say that Christ will reign through you? *No!* Rather, it says that you will reign (in this life) through Christ. *How do you reign? By using your faith, with corresponding actions!* You are now seated with Christ at God's right hand. *So, what are you doing with what you have received?* (Ephesians 2:6, James 2:17)

For whatever is born of God overcomes the world. And this is the victory that has overcome the world—our faith.
– 1 John 5:4

Prayer: *Heavenly Father, I thank You for the abundance of grace that I have received through Christ. I also thank You for the gift of righteousness. I refuse to be a victim in life. I choose to use my faith to reign in life through Jesus Christ.*

August 16
BE THANKFUL

Bless the Lord, O my soul; And all that is within me, *bless* His holy name! Bless the Lord, O my soul, And forget not all His benefits. – Psalm 103:1-2

Thanksgiving is the lifestyle of winners! This is because they recognise the value of what God has done in times past, what He is doing currently, and what He will do in the future. Even when things are not going well, God remains faithful and true. *He is mighty to save and He is the God of all comfort and restoration.* The fact that you are alive is enough reason for being thankful. It is commonly said that: *'when there is life, there is hope'*. Consider the many times that God has delivered your life from destruction. He forgives all your sins and crowns you with tender mercies (Isaiah 38:18-19, Ecclesiastes 9:4, 2 Corinthians 1:3-5).

The Bible does not promise us that 'life is a bed of roses'. We will go through some trials and persecutions in this life. We will go through some times of difficulty or uncertainty. *However, the Lord has promised that He will never leave nor forsake us.* Therefore, you can still bless His Name, even on the road marked with suffering. *Psalm 84:6-7* refers to those who passing through the dry sunless valley of weeping, make it a place of springs and rejoicing. They choose to praise the Lord, irrespective of circumstances! *Unthankfulness is a symptom of pride and selfishness!* People are unthankful because they have an attitude of entitlement. *We are to live thankfully!* (Hebrews 13:5)

Confession: *I have confidence in my Heavenly Father. He is the God who is more than enough. I choose to be thankful in life. I refuse to be proud and selfish. I express gratitude to God always and I live thankfully, in Jesus' Name. Amen.*

August 17
RAISED AND SEATED

... according to the working of His mighty power which He worked in Christ when He raised Him from the dead and seated Him at His right hand in the heavenly places, far above all principality and power and might and dominion, and every name that is named, not only in this age but also in that which is to come. – Ephesians 1:19-21

On the third day (Easter Sunday, Firstfruits), *Jesus Christ was resurrected by the Heavenly Father, as the firstborn from the dead, with a new celestial body*. He conquered Sin, darkness (spiritual death) and physical death. The resurrection of Jesus Christ is an historical fact which will easily sail through any trial and jury in our modern legal systems. His tomb was found empty despite having been heavily guarded by Roman soldiers. He was seen by over 500 witnesses over the next 40 days in different places within Israel, after which He literally ascended into the highest Heaven in the presence of some of these witnesses at the mount called Olivet. *Jesus Christ is now seated at the right hand of the Father in Heaven, until all His enemies are put under*. The disciples who were sore afraid after His crucifixion became bold after His resurrection, ascension and the Pentecost. Therefore, from a team of 120 grew a Christian church that has reached the very ends of the world despite intense persecution from the Jewish leaders and the Roman Empire of that day. Many of them were willing to die for their faith in Jesus Christ (Psalm 110:1-7).

Prayer: Thank You Lord for coming 'down to earth' to lay down Your life as the eternal sacrifice for Sin. Thank You for bearing my Sin and all of its consequences. Thank You for the free gift of eternal life which is dominating me now.

August 18
SPIRITUAL UNDERSTANDING

For this reason we also, since the day we heard it, do not cease to pray for you, and to ask that you may be filled with the knowledge of His will in all wisdom and spiritual understanding; that you may walk worthy of the Lord, fully pleasing *Him,* being fruitful in every good work and increasing in the knowledge of God. – Colossians 1:9-10

Do you desire to walk worthy of the Lord and to be fully pleasing to Him? Do you desire to be fruitful in every good work and to increase in your knowledge of God? If so, you need to be filled with the knowledge of His will. *Ephesians 5:17* shows us that it is foolish not to understand what the will of the Lord is. *Hosea 4:6* says that 'God's people' are destroyed for lack of knowledge (Ephesians 4:18).

How can you be filled with the knowledge of His will? The answer is: 'through light and understanding'. The reason why some people are living foolishly, or under oppression of the devil, is due to a lack of 'light and understanding'. The enlightenment of your understanding refers to your heart being <u>flooded with divine light</u> (Ephesians 1:17-19).

How can you get spiritual light and understanding? You are to study and pray for it! You should <u>fervently desire</u> and pray to your *Father* to fill you with spiritual wisdom and understanding on a regular basis. Moreover, you should <u>give attention</u> to His Word daily, with an attitude of humility and obedience. *Don't forget that the entrance of His Word brings light and understanding* (Psalm 119:130).

Confession: *I am a child of light and I belong to the body of Christ. Spiritual wisdom and understanding is dominating my life. I refuse to walk in darkness. I walk in the light by studying the Word and fellowshipping with true believers.*

August 19
GOD AND MONEY

No one can serve two masters; for either he will hate the one and love the other, or else he will be loyal to the one and despise the other. You cannot serve God and mammon.
– Matthew 6:24

The foundational step to your Christian service is paying your tithes (i.e. 10% of your income) to your local church. Are you in financial partnership with God? Are you worshipping God with your money? What percentage of your income do you think that God's work deserves? *Giving generously is not about numbers. It is about percentages.* Tithing is the starting point (training wheels) of generous giving (Malachi 3:10, 2 Corinthians 9:6).

Your tithe is not optional; it is an act of obedience and gratitude, with expectation of blessing. Christians need to understand that the devil is very keen to hinder the work of God on the earth, and a major way to do this is by getting them to withhold their tithes, for this deprives the local church of a regular income for doing the Lord's work. Why should you spend more money on 'restaurants and tips' than you give to your Lord? Why should you spend more money on 'clothes, toys and entertainment' than you give to your Lord? Actually, we haven't really given until we've paid our tithes. *Tithing is not the last word in generosity; it's the first word.* You should pay your tithe where you receive spiritual nourishment (e.g. your local church). You should also give offerings above your tithes.

Prayer: *Almighty God, I thank You for all You have given me. There is nothing I have that I have not received. Help me to serve you faithfully with my money. Help to me to be faithful in tithes and offerings, in Jesus' Name. Amen.*

August 20
POWER OF FELLOWSHIP

"Again I say to you that if two of you agree on earth concerning anything that they ask, it will be done for them by My Father in heaven. For where two or three are gathered together in My name, I am there in the midst of them."
– Matthew 18:19-20

The Lord Jesus said that where two or three are gathered together in His Name, He is there in their midst. What does this mean? *It refers to the power of fellowship.* Of course, we know that God is everywhere. However, whenever we gather together in fellowship with other true believers *in the Name of Jesus*, the presence and power of God is more strongly revealed. Whenever believers gather together in genuine fellowship, *the anointing (yoke-destroying and burden-removing power) of the Holy Spirit* is released to do greater things in their midst (Psalm 133, Acts 2:1-4).

Your fellowship with other believers is your cooperate act of worship. The church is the body of Christ and if you are a Christian, you belong to this body. You cannot make substantial spiritual progress without *genuine fellowship* and *inspiring leadership*. It is not enough to attend church on Sundays only. Other church meetings such as *home groups, bible study, prayer meeting, evangelism and socials* are very important because they contribute significantly to your growth. Don't keep away from church meetings! You need to rub off with other believers, in order to grow. *You need church, and the church needs you!* (Hebrews 10:25).

Confession: *I am a child of God and my life is governed by the Word. I refuse to be rebellious! I am fully committed to church and consistent in attendance. I submit to genuine fellowship and inspiring church leadership, in Jesus' Name.*

August 21
THE ORIGINAL SIN

And the Lord God commanded the man, saying, "Of every tree of the garden you may freely eat; but of the tree of the knowledge of good and evil you shall not eat, for in the day that you eat of it you shall surely die."
– Genesis 2:16-17

In *Genesis 3*, we read the unfortunate story of the fall of man. The original sin was not just 'eating a forbidden fruit'. Rather, it involved *selfishness and rebellion* against God. Eve was deceived by the serpent (Satan) into desiring *the knowledge of good and evil*. She expected that knowledge to make her wise, evolved and independent. However, Adam was not deceived (1 Timothy 2:13-14). He knew fully well what Eve had done and the resulting consequence of death. However, he was not willing to lose Eve, who had become the most precious thing to him on the earth.

The real test was this: Adam had to choose between Eve and God; between the created and the creator. *The forbidden fruit is a test of true worship; the ultimate test of allegiance that determined the fall*. Adam chose to die with Eve rather than to live with God alone. *The original sin is 'selfishness and rebellion'*. What is taking the place of God in your life today? What is taking away your time, talents, resources and money, in the place of God? You need to repent of all such idolatry today and give your complete allegiance to God. *You are to love the Lord your God with all your heart: that is the first commandment!* (Mark 12:30)

Prayer: *Dear Heavenly Father, I thank You because You have loved me with an everlasting love. Help me to know You more. Help me to see You more clearly, love You more dearly and follow You more nearly, in Jesus' Name. Amen.*

August 22
GREAT TRIBULATION

For then there will be great tribulation, such as has not been since the beginning of the world until this time, no, nor ever shall be. And unless those days were shortened, no flesh would be saved ... – Matthew 24:21-22

The tribulation is a 7-year period of unparalleled turmoil on the whole earth, for at this time the judgements of God are poured on a rebellious world and the man of Sin, the antichrist, is allowed to reign over the nations of the earth. The tribulation is triggered by the rapture of the saints, for the Spirit-filled church is the restraining factor on the full explosion of evil in our world today. The Day of the Lord (*Rapture–Tribulation–Armageddon–Millennium*) so comes (begins) as a thief in the night (1 Thessalonians 5:1-10).

Those who are *left behind* after the rapture of the saints are unbelievers and false believers. This includes all those who have not made Jesus Christ the Lord of their lives, and those who have departed from the faith by giving heed to the lies of Satan. The apostate church (the church of the Laodiceans) consists of lukewarm unbelievers: which are false believers. *Don't be left behind!* (Revelations 3:14-22).

For the mystery of lawlessness is already at work; only He who now restrains will do so until He is taken out of the way. And then the lawless one will be revealed, whom the Lord will consume with the breath of His mouth and destroy with the brightness of His coming. – 2 Thessalonians 2:7-8

Confession: *The Rapture is the Blessed Hope of true believers in Christ. In the twinkling of an eye, we shall be translated up to Heaven. I will continue to abide faithfully in Christ, and I will not be found wanting when He returns.*

August 23
GET BEHIND ME

Then Peter took Him aside and began to rebuke Him, saying, "Far be it from You, Lord; this shall not happen to You!" But He turned and said to Peter, "Get behind Me, Satan! You are an offense to Me, for you are not mindful of the things of God, but the things of men." – Matthew 16:22-23

People have free will and can yield to either God or the devil at various times. We see an excellent example of this in *Matthew 16:13-23*. At first, Simon Peter yielded to Holy Spirit in saying that 'Jesus is the Christ, the son of the living God'. Not long thereafter, Jesus began to talk about His impending death and resurrection. In this instance, Peter yielded to Satan and began to rebuke Jesus from going to the Cross. Jesus replied: 'Get behind Me, Satan!' *Jesus wasn't calling Peter a devil. No! Rather He was taking authority over Satan*. He was showing that Peter had sided in with the devil, through doubt and fear (Ephesians 4:27). *Careless Christians can yield (unconsciously) to the devil at various times*. Satan can make use of <u>unbelievers and carnal Christians</u> to cause 'confusion and trouble' in the home, church or workplace. However, we have authority over Satan and his demons, <u>in the Name of Jesus</u>. You have authority over the forces of darkness. *You can exercise spiritual authority over others, when they are yielding to the devil*. You claim your authority and calmly rebuke the evil spirits involved. *You command them to stop in their operations – and the situation must change!* (James 4:7)

Prayer: *Almighty and Everlasting God, I thank You that I have authority over devils in the Name of Jesus. I refuse to be manipulated by demonic spirits. I exercise my spiritual authority at home, church and work, in Jesus' Name. Amen.*

August 24
THE SAFEST PLACE

Abide in Me, and I in you. As the branch cannot bear fruit of itself, unless it abides in the vine, neither can you, unless you abide in Me … If anyone does not abide in Me, he is cast out as a branch and is withered; and they gather them and throw *them* into the fire, and they are burned. – John 15:4-6

The safest place on earth for any man to dwell is in the centre of God's will. Abiding in Him is the <u>most intelligent</u> thing you can do with your life. *God's Word is God's will*. When God speaks, He is giving you inside information for your advantage, and your obedience is the <u>most profitable</u> thing you could do for yourself. *His will may be demanding and challenging. However, it is ultimately most rewarding*. Walking away from God's will for your life will make you vulnerable to the dirty tricks of the devil. *Humility and obedience will help you go far in this life* (James 4:6).

Living outside the will of God may seem smart, pleasant and fun-filled in the short-term. However, it always leads to trouble and heartache. <u>Remember Lot</u> in *Genesis 13 and Genesis 19*. He drifted towards the land of Sodom, because it looked like a well-watered garden. However, he ended up losing everything he valued when Sodom was destroyed because of sin and immorality. *The most dangerous place for any Christian to be is outside God's will*. In such a place, it easy for Satan to get them and cut short their lives. Learn to yield to the Word and Spirit. Learn to repent quickly and realign yourself. *The centre of His will is your safest place!*

Confession: *I am a child of Wisdom and I refuse to live foolishly. I choose to live in the centre of God's will. I refuse to be rebellious. I abide in Him. He is the vine and I am the branch. I embrace humility and obedience, in Jesus' Name.*

August 25
FAITHFUL SERVICE

Let a man so consider us, as servants of Christ and stewards of the mysteries of God. Moreover it is required in stewards that one be found faithful. – 1 Corinthians 4:1-2

The watchword of Christian service is faithfulness. The Lord's servants (i.e. all true Christians) are expected to serve Him. God never demands too much and He rewards those that diligently seek Him. *The parable of the talents* refers to faithfulness in Christian service (Matthew 25:14-30, Luke 19:11-27). Note that all your abilities come from God; you are nothing without Him (James 1:17). *Talents* are opportunities to use our natural and spiritual abilities to serve the Lord. *Time is a precious gift from God: Use it wisely!* The time to serve God is now. You have to invest the opportunities that you have now to serve God now.

Don't wait for big opportunities. Your service to the Lord usually starts with little things. In fact, nothing is too small. The little things that you do now will open the door for greater opportunities in the future. *It is faithfulness that God rewards, not position.* Whatever your daily occupation is, you can use it to honour and glorify God. You can serve God in your workplace with what you say and what you do, on a daily basis. Don't compromise your identity as a true disciple of Christ. *The eternal status and spiritual maturity of many souls depend on your faithful service to the Lord.* Most importantly, your service brings glory to God and an overflow of divine blessings to you (Exodus 23:25-26).

Prayer: *Dear Heavenly Father, I rededicate myself to You. I desire to serve You faithfully. Help me to use my abilities to move Your church forward. Help me to be committed to service and supportive of the church, in Jesus' Name. Amen*

August 26
DRESSED OR UNDRESSED?

Then the Lord God called to Adam and said to him, "Where *are* you?" So he said, "I heard Your voice in the garden, and I was afraid because I was naked; and I hid myself." And He said, "Who told you that you *were* naked? Have you eaten from the tree of which I commanded you … not eat?" – Genesis 3:9-11

Have you ever wondered why people have to wear clothes at all? Wouldn't it be easier and cheaper if we all walked around stark naked (assuming there is no harsh weather)? When Adam and Eve sinned, they *fell short* of the glory of God. That glory had provided a covering for them, but when it departed, they saw their nakedness and felt newly the emotions of shame and fear. Since then, the flesh has remained in a *fallen perishable state* and will only be redeemed (glorified) at the Rapture (resurrection) of true believers in Christ (Romans 3:23, 1 Corinthians 15:42-58). The stronghold of 'sin and death' is in the flesh (Romans 7:23, 8:3), and a primary force that we will contend with throughout life is the lust of the flesh. *We put on clothes in order to hide our nakedness and restrain the power of lust*. This lustful power lies in the exposure of fresh, smooth, delicate, shiny or tightly-fitted skin. Be careful to keep your private parts '*private*'. Keep your private regions (genitals, buttocks, breasts and armpits) well covered in public. *Anytime you dress up, consider whether you are an agent of lust or godliness*. Dressing properly is an act of worship to God. *Look in the mirror: are you dressed or undressed?*

Confession: *My body is the temple of the Holy Spirit. My body belongs to the Lord. I will glorify God with my body. I refuse careless or foolish dressing. I embrace proper and decent dressing. I embrace inner beauty, in Jesus' Name.*

August 27
SUBJECT YOUR BODY

Therefore I run thus: not with uncertainty. Thus I fight: not as *one who* beats the air. But I discipline my body and bring *it* into subjection, lest, when I have preached to others, I myself should become disqualified. – 1 Corinthians 9:26-27

Your body is your outward man; the house that your inner man (spirit and soul) lives in. *Although your spirit is saved and your soul is being saved, your body is still mortal*. It is subject to temptation and carnal desires. Therefore, it is important that you are spirit-ruled rather than being body-ruled. *If you want to live victoriously and fulfil the eternal purposes of God for your life, you have to subject your body to the supremacy of your spirit*. This always involves diligence and discipline. An undisciplined Christian will waste a lot of God-given opportunities due to laziness and carelessness. Grace does not permit you to be lazy and careless. Rather it empowers to do all things through Christ who strengthens you (Romans 8:5-8, Philippians 4:13).

You subject your body by 'walking in the Spirit'. *Your walk in the Spirit is a function of 'training and practice'*. You will only move forward spiritually in accordance with your *progressive acts of obedience*. You cannot afford to always give in to your body's desires, such as entertainment and relaxation. *Don't overeat, overplay or oversleep your life away.* Be diligent to present yourself approved unto God, a worker with no shame. *You cannot walk in God's will if you always give in to feelings and emotions!* (2 Timothy 2:15)

Prayer: *Dear Father in Heaven, I rededicate myself to You. I subject my body to the supremacy of my spirit, always. Help me to make use of every opportunity I have to do Your will. Help me to be diligent and disciplined, in Jesus' Name.*

August 28
PRAYER OF AGREEMENT

"Again I say to you that if two of you agree on earth concerning anything that they ask, it will be done for them by My Father in heaven. For where two or three are gathered together in My name, I am there in the midst of them."
− Matthew 18:19-20

Every true believer has been called into a lifetime of prayer and study. You simply cannot afford to be 'prayerless' in this ungodly generation. *You cannot afford to be so busy that you don't have time for prayer and the Word, daily.* Some people say that it doesn't matter how you pray; that all prayers are the same. Really? Are all types of food the same in their effect on your body? Do you want to remain a spiritual baby forever? The Bible shows us that there are different types of prayer for different purposes. *A good study of the Word will help you to make the most of your prayer life.* We are to 'watch and pray' (1 John 5:14-15).

There are times when your faith alone is not sufficient to carry you through. This is why *Ecclesiastes 4:9* says that two are better than one. *The prayer of agreement has to do with joining your faith with that of another; it is based on a unity of purpose.* When two believers agree together concerning anything that they ask, it will be done for them by *the Father.* The power of agreement is so tremendous in relationship to what God can do, that it brings about exponential increase. *For if one can chase a thousand, two will chase ten thousand,* as shown in *Deuteronomy 32:30.*

Confession: *I am a child of God and I have access to His throne in the Name of Jesus. I commit to a lifestyle of prayer and study. I refuse to be lazy! I take advantage of the power of agreement in prayer, in Jesus' Name. Amen.*

August 29
YOU HAVE PATIENCE

But the fruit of the Spirit is love, joy, peace, longsuffering, kindness, goodness, faithfulness, gentleness, self-control. Against such there is no law. – Galatians 5:22-23

The fruit of the Spirit is love (longsuffering, gentleness and self-control). *The fruit of the Spirit simply means the fruit that the Holy Spirit helps your human spirit to produce.* If you are born-again, you have the full capacity to produce the fruit of love, because God's love has been shed abroad in your heart by His Spirit (Romans 5:5). The first definition of love in *1 Corinthians 13* is: *Love is patient and kind!* This means that impatience is a major work of the sinful nature. Patience is a complex virtue that usually involves *self-control, humility and generosity*. It usually involves self-restraint, the laying down of your right to anger and protest, and a willingness to be large-hearted. It is said that '*patience is the greatest of all virtues*' (James 1:2-4).

The Bible tells us of how people lost their blessings due to impatience. In *1 Samuel 13*, King Saul was so impatient for Samuel, he went ahead to perform the priestly sacrifice. He lost his kingdom as a result. In *Exodus 32*, the Israelites were so impatient for Moses, they committed idolatry by worshipping a gold calf. 3,000 people lost their lives and many were plagued as a result. *How do you overcome impatience? Walk in the Spirit!* Allow the Holy Spirit to guide your life. Embrace humility and obedience. Walk in love. *Walk by faith, and not by sight!* (2 Corinthians 5:7)

Prayer: Almighty God, thank You for Your compassion and mercy. Thank You for always bearing with me, even in my weaknesses. Help me to give freely the love I have received. Help me to be patient and kind, in Jesus' Name. Amen.

August 30
HELP FROM ABOVE

I will lift up my eyes to the hills—
From whence comes my help?
My help *comes* from the Lord,
Who made heaven and earth.
− Psalm 121:1-2

For the natural man, life is full of 'ups and downs'. Many go through times when they feel low. At such times, it is indeed possible to feel lonely in the midst of many people. However, this does not have to be the case for the spiritual man. *Your inner state is not a function of circumstances; it is mainly a function of what you are looking at*. If you keep looking at circumstances, you will end up discouraged. *Determine not to look around; instead look up!* Lift up your eyes to the hill of Calvary and consider Jesus Christ who has paid the price for you. He has redeemed you from the curse, so that you can enjoy The BLESSING (Galatians 3:13). *Where does your help come from? Is it worth it to look up to man?* The problem with humans is that they are not always reliable or available. They are also limited in ability. No wonder the Bible says that vain is the help of man (Psalm 60:11-12). *Your help comes from the Lord who made all things! Isn't that so reassuring?* God is able to raise up kings for your sake, as you abide in His Word. He is able to suspend the laws of nature for your sake, as you abide in His Will (His Word is His Will*). Lift up your eyes to Him in faith and thanksgiving. He will help!* (Hebrews 11:6).

Confession: *I have been justified by faith and I have peace with God. What a tremendous treasure! I refuse to be downcast! I lift up my eyes to the Lord in faith, praise and thanksgiving. He will surely help me, in Jesus' Name. Amen*

August 31
MORE THAN CONQUERORS

Who shall separate us from the love of Christ? *Shall*
tribulation, or distress, or persecution, or famine, or
nakedness, or peril, or sword?
Yet in all these things we are more than conquerors through
Him who loved us. – Romans 8:35,37

Life is not balanced, but God is faithful. No matter what
hard time you are going through today, it is not going to be
forever. This is because the love of God towards you is
everlasting. *Lamentations 3:22-23* makes us to understand
that the steadfast love of the lord never ceases and His
mercies never come to an end. *Don't keep looking around;*
all you need do is to keep looking up to Him, for He is ever
faithful and true to His Word. No matter what challenge
life throws at you, God is able to see you through and take
you over. *His love is unfailing and His mercies endure*.
What shall separate you from the love of Christ? Is it
persecution, bereavement, lack or disappointment from
others? No! You cannot be angry with God. *Jeremiah 29:11*
says that His thoughts towards you are of peace, not of evil
Although life may throw different challenges, *Jesus is the*
friend that sticks closer than a brother. He has promised to
never leave nor forsake you. *No matter what you are going*
through, learn to give thanks! Because of God's love, you
already have Zoe (the divine overcoming life) within you.
Therefore, you are indeed more than a conqueror in all
these things (Proverbs 18:24, 1 Thessalonians 5:18).

Prayer: *Father God, thank You for Your everlasting love.*
Thank You because Your love is steadfast and Your mercies
are sure. Thank You because Your plans towards me are of
peace. I am more than a conqueror, in Jesus' Name. Amen.

September 1
ASK WHAT YOU WILL

If you abide in Me, and My words abide in you, you will ask what you desire, and it shall be done for you.
– John 15:7

I don't understand why some Christians want to have as little as possible to do with Jesus Christ and His Church! As a true believer, you are to abide (dwell) in Christ. *He is the true vine and we are His branches*! Some people have their daily routine so figured out, with little room for God. They have planned (or unplanned) their lives so well, and carved out their pathway to success and greatness in life without taking into account *the will and purposes of God*. They seem to have forgotten that unless the Lord builds the house, the workers are *labouring in vain*. If you abide in Christ, you will bear good fruit, for *without Him you can do nothing* of eternal value (Psalm 127:1, John 15:5).

When you delight yourself in the Lord, He will give you the desires of your heart *in a much better way* (Psalm 37:4). *How you do delight yourself in Him? You do this by abiding in His Word.* God's Word is God's Will. Devote quality time to 'reading and meditating' on God's Word daily. Let the Word dominate <u>your mouth</u>. Be careful to live your life in line with the Word. *Spend time in genuine fellowship with true believers.* <u>Let the Word be the final authority in your life</u>. As you do this, you will begin to understand the mind of God and His will. *When the Word dominates your life, <u>you will ask</u> whatever you desire and <u>it will be done</u> for you*.

Prayer: *Almighty God, without You, I can do nothing. I'm sorry for not giving proper attention to the Word. I choose to abide in Your Word. I receive grace to live by the Word, and confidence to ask what I desire, in Jesus' Name. Amen.*

September 2
DIVINE SUBSTITUTION

For He made Him who knew no sin to be sin for us, that we might become the righteousness of God in Him.
– 2 Corinthians 5:21

Jesus Christ became Sin for us, so that we can become Righteousness. We access this by faith when we accept Him as *Saviour*, believe that we are forgiven and cleansed by His blood, and proclaim that we are saved.

that it might be fulfilled which was spoken by Isaiah the prophet, saying: "He Himself took our infirmities And bore our sicknesses." – Matthew 8:17

Jesus Christ became Sickness for us, so that we can become Health. We access this by faith when we accept Him as *Healer*, believe that we have been healed by His wounds, and proclaim that we are healed and healthy.

For you know the grace of our Lord Jesus Christ, that though He was rich, yet for your sakes He became poor, that you through His poverty might become rich. – 2 Corinthians 8:9

Jesus Christ became Poverty for us, so that we can become abundantly supplied. We access this by faith when we accept Him as *Provider*, believe that we have been delivered from poverty by His lack on the cross, give generously, and proclaim that we are abundantly supplied.

Confession: I am the righteousness of God in Christ Jesus: sin has no dominion over me! Himself took my infirmities and bore my sicknesses: I live in divine health and healing! He became poor so I can be rich: I am abundantly supplied!

September 3
EXERCISE YOUR FAITH

**What *does it* profit, my brethren, if someone says he has faith
but does not have works? Can faith save him?
For as the body without the spirit is dead, so faith without
works is dead also.** – James 1:14,26

*If you leave your muscles unexercised for an extended
period of time, they will become stiff and ineffective.* This
same principle applies to faith. The first step is to feed on
the Word through study and fellowship. However, feeding
alone is not enough. *You have to exercise your faith by
putting it into use daily.* Faith without corresponding
actions is useless! *Your words and actions must correspond
to what you believe.* For example, if you are born-again,
you need to declare it, and live out a godly life. If you want
'great' faith, start by exercising your 'little' faith. *Plant your
mustard seed faith (by exercising it) and it will grow to
move mountains* (2 Thessalonians 1:3, Matthew 17:20).
If you always jump at finding natural solutions to all your
problems in life, how will you ever learn to walk in the
supernatural? Thank God for the good work of medicine
and doctors. *However, is your faith in the Word bigger
than your faith in medicine?* When you have a little
problem (e.g. mere headache), boldly rebuke it and claim
your victory (healing) in the Name of Jesus. Then believe
that it is done, and ignore the symptoms by a continuous
confession of faith and thanksgiving. *I tell you the truth,
you will have what you believe and say!* (Mark 11:22-24)

Prayer: *Dear Father, I thank You for the triumphant victory
of Christ at the cross. I rejoice that I can stand firm in that
victory by faith. I refuse to be lazy and unbelieving. Help me
to diligently exercise my faith daily, in Jesus' Name. Amen.*

September 4
WORRY FOR NOTHING

Be anxious for nothing, but in everything by prayer and supplication, with thanksgiving, let your requests be made known to God; and the peace of God, which surpasses all understanding, will guard your hearts and minds through Christ Jesus. – Philippians 4:6-7

Do you want to live in a constant state of inner peace and good health? If so, you must be anxious for nothing. The amplified version of today's verse says: Do not fret or have any anxiety about anything! *Is it really possible to live without worry?* You can achieve a 'worryless' life if you learn to focus on God. *Worry is a vote of no confidence in God!* The Bibles says that we are to cast all our cares upon Him, for He cares for us. All true believers in Christ are <u>commanded</u> 'not to worry' (1 Peter 5:7, Matthew 6:25).
Life is full of many different challenges and the temptation to worry is always present. God has given you a sound mind (2 Timothy 1:7) which will alert you to problems and dangers. When alerted, the proper thing is to take action accordingly, as led by the Spirit of God. In this regard, your concern is appropriate. However, beware of becoming over-concerned. *Worry has to do with situations that you can do nothing about in the present.* At these times, you must learn to trust God for His help and guidance. *Take it to the Lord in prayer and leave it there.* Rather than worrying, practice a confession of faith, with praise and thanksgiving. *Learn to stay your mind on Him!* (Isaiah 26:3)

Confession: *God has given me a sound mind and I use it to take appropriate action when needed. However, I refuse to fear or worry. I subscribe to prayer and thanksgiving. I have confidence in God to help and guide me, in Jesus' Name.*

September 5
DO YOU LOVE ME?

**So when they had eaten breakfast, Jesus said to Simon Peter,
"Simon, *son* of Jonah, do you love Me more than these?"
He said to Him, "Yes, Lord; You know that I love You."
He said to him, "Feed My lambs." – John 21:15**

In *John 21*, we read the story of Peter who went fishing in the Sea of Tiberias with six other disciples. Recall that Jesus had called these disciples to leave commercial fishing to become fishers of men. Maybe Peter went fishing because he got bored of Jesus being no longer physically present with them. However, the reality is that he was <u>backsliding</u> away from kingdom business. Think of what would have happened if Jesus had not intervened. Their commercial fishing business would have resurrected, in the place of their higher calling to preach the gospel. <u>How pathetic!</u>
The true test of discipleship is discipline with regard to your calling. The true test of love is devotion and obedience. In restoring Peter, Jesus asked him the question 'Do you love Me?' three times. Don't forget that Peter had also denied Jesus three times at the time of His suffering. The correct answer to that question is found in *John 14:15*, which says: 'If you love me, you will keep (obey) my commandments'. *Loving God is not just about pleasant emotions. It is more about devotion and obedience.* If you love God, you will give priority to the things of God. This includes attendance and punctuality to church meetings, giving, serving and evangelism. *Do you really love him?* (Matthew 28:18-20).

Prayer: *Almighty God, I thank You for Your gracious and compassionate love. Thank you for saving me from spiritual and eternal death. As I have received Your love freely, help me to respond in devotion and obedience, in Jesus' Name.*

September 6
GOD REFLECTED

**"You are worthy, O Lord, To receive glory and honour and
power; For You created all things,
And by Your will they exist and were created."**
– Revelation 4:11

The Most High is the source of life, light and love. He has a
vision (worship) and a mission (redemption). He is faithful,
righteous, holy and just. He is also patient and merciful.
Notice that all the attributes of the Most High are relevant
to man. *Man mirrors and shadows the Most High*. He
desires power and dominion. He resists defeat and seeks
to rule over his world. He fights wars in order to preserve
his freedom. *He desires light and development*. He makes
inventions and works hard to improve his quality of life.
He makes definite plans based on definite purposes and
has the innate capacity to envision and do great things. He
desires social relationships as reflected in family, friends,
and societies. *Man desires moral uprightness, cleanliness,
and beauty* as reflected in character references, reward
systems, hygiene ratings, fashion, cosmetics, lights and
fireworks. *Man desires to love and be loved*. He desires
forgiveness and mercy as reflected in official pardons and
royal prerogatives of mercy. *Man desires a just, fair and
smooth-running society*. Therefore men make laws to
govern, expect compliance and apply corresponding
punishment to offenders. *It is even asserted that ignorance
is not an excuse in law* (Genesis 1:27, Romans 1:20).

Confession: *I am recreated in the likeness of God. I am just
like Him. Zoe, the life of God, flows in me. I have a new
nature and a new identity. The light of God shines through
me. His love dominates me and His faith works in my life.*

September 7
BE CONTINUOSLY FILLED

And do not be drunk with wine, in which is dissipation; but be filled with the Spirit, speaking to one another in psalms and hymns and spiritual songs, singing and making melody in your heart to the Lord – Ephesians 5:18-19

In *John 7:37*, Jesus Christ shouted to the crowd: "*If anyone thirsts, let him come to Me and drink.*" He was referring to being filled with the Holy Spirit. Note that you cannot receive the Holy Spirit baptism if you are not thirsty for Him. Furthermore, *John 7:38-39* shows us that the fullness of the Spirit is reserved for only those who believe and have received Jesus as their personal Lord and Saviour. *Are you thirsty for more of God?* If this is so, what have you been drinking? Have you been drinking of the Holy Spirit? *Do not become intoxicated by the desire for or dominion of alcohol, for the Bible calls alcohol a destroyer* (Proverbs 23:31-32, 20:1). The Bible commands us to be filled with the Spirit. *Alcohol is false wine; the Holy Spirit is true wine.* Holy Spirit baptism is evidenced by the outward sign of 'speaking in unknown tongues', which is an overflow of the indwelling Spirit. The Spirit gives the utterance from our innermost being and *we do the speaking,* by faith (Acts 2:4, 10:45-46). Speaking in tongues is a 'river of living water' that releases supernatural power into your life. *How can you stay filled? Keep drinking by speaking in tongues!* Pray in tongues consistently. Speak psalms, hymns and spiritual songs in tongues. *Make melody in your heart to the Lord.*

Confession: *I have the Spirit of the living God dwelling in me. I choose to be full of the Word and full of the Spirit. I drink of the Spirit by speaking in tongues. I pray and sing with tongues to release the supernatural upon my world.*

September 8
TONGUES AND PROPHECY

He who speaks in a tongue edifies himself, but he who prophesies edifies the church. I wish you all spoke with tongues, but even more that you prophesied; for he who prophesies *is* greater than he who speaks with tongues, unless indeed he interprets, that the church may receive edification.
– 1 Corinthians 14:4-5

Spiritual gifts help to equip believers to function properly in fellowship and evangelism. *We cannot afford to be ignorant regarding spiritual gifts because they are for our own good*. You have to desire these gifts in your life (1 Corinthians 12). The *gifts of utterance* include *prophecy* (inspired message), *diverse tongues* (inspired message in unknown language) and *interpretation of tongues* (inspired interpretation of tongues). The *general gift of tongues* is given to every believer as a confirming sign of the Holy Spirit baptism (Acts 2:4). These tongues are for *personal edification* in prayer. However, there is also the *specific gift of diverse tongues* for the purpose of *prophecy: an inspired utterance for exhortation and encouragement of believers*.

In this regard, all believers can prophesy as led by the Holy Spirit. *Note that prophesying does not make you a prophet, unless with accompanying gifts of revelation*. Believers can be given a message in tongues, but it will be of no use unless someone interprets it in plain language. This is why *prophecy in tongues* must be accompanied by the *gift of interpretation*, whether from the same person or another.

Confession: *The Spirit of the living God dwells within me. I believe I receive the fullness of the Spirit. I desire the gifts of prophecy, diverse tongues and interpretation of tongues, to edify the church. I believe I receive them, in Jesus' Name.*

September 9
BEAUTY IS VAIN

Charm *is* deceitful and beauty *is* passing,
But a woman *who* fears the Lord, she shall be praised.
Give her of the fruit of her hands,
And let her own works praise her in the gates.
– Proverbs 31:30-31

If you are seeking for a good wife or husband, the most important qualification is not their outward beauty. Don't be carried away by how they look or dress. Many people are beautiful outside (either naturally or artificially) but they are proud, mean, selfish or rotten inside. *Some people are actually beautiful Jezebels or charming devils.* The most important quality of an excellent life partner is the fear of the Lord. *The reverent and worshipful fear of the Lord is the choicest part of Wisdom* (Proverbs 7:10-11, 9:10).

Did you know that outward beauty fades away with age? Do you know that charm can be a presentation to impress? *Many people revert to their bad (and hidden) habits once they are well-settled in a long-term relationship.* Inner beauty is based on the fear of the Lord. The fear the Lord helps you to walk in humility towards your spouse. It helps you to stay faithful in the good times and bad. It helps you to be diligent at home, knowing that your service to your family is a service to the Lord. It helps you to pay attention to the things of God, including attendance and punctuality to church meetings. *A (wo)man who fears the Lord shall be praised. Their works will praise them in the gates!*

Prayer: *Dear Father in Heaven, thank You for Your holy written Word which has the power to renew my mind. I refuse to be selfish and stubborn. Help me to fully embrace the fear of the Lord. Help me to be faithful, in Jesus' Name.*

September 10
WE HAVE AN ADVOCATE

My little children, these things I write to you, so that you may not sin. And if anyone sins, we have an Advocate with the Father, Jesus Christ the righteous. – 1 John 2:1

Do Christians sin? Yes, of course, for they are still living inside the fallen flesh. *But I thought that true believers in Christ are called Saints?* Yes, believers are called Saints because they have been washed and made right with God through the precious blood of Jesus. *They have received the gift of Righteousness!* (1 Corinthians 1:2, Romans 5:17) As believers, it is important to know that we have an *Advocate* with the *Father*. An advocate (lawyer) is one who stands in your place to plead your case. *Jesus Christ (The Righteous One) is the sinning Christian's advocate*. This is not a licence to sin; rather it is a licence to Righteousness. Now, if you are truly born-again, then you don't want to sin. You don't want to lie or steal or fight or cheat. *The 'wanting to' is gone, because your spirit is a new creation!* (2 Corinthians 5:17). However, you still get tempted to do wrong things because of your flesh (which is a combination of your <u>unrenewed mind</u> and <u>unglorified body</u>). When you do wrong, <u>run to God</u>, confess your sin and ask for His forgiveness. He is 'faithful and just' to forgive you, and to cleanse you from all unrighteousness (1 John 1:9). Don't allow the devil to subject you to condemnation. *If you have <u>repented</u> of it, then you can be sure that God has cast it into His Sea of Forgetfulness* (Micah 7:19, Isaiah 43:25).

Confession: *I have been made right with God through the precious blood of Jesus. He is my Advocate with the Father whenever I sin. I am not under divine condemnation! I am quick to repent! My sins are in God's Sea of Forgetfulness.*

September 11
BE TEACHABLE

Likewise you younger people, submit yourselves to *your* elders. Yes, all of *you* be submissive to one another, and be clothed with humility, for "God resists the proud, But gives grace to the humble."
− 1 Peter 5:5

Matthew 25:31-46 speaks about the parable of the sheep and the goats. Although sheep and goats have many similarities, they also have outstanding differences. Goats are curious and stubborn, while sheep are trusting and submissive. *Goats tend to stray away while sheep tend to flock together*. The Bible calls Jesus the *Chief Shepherd* and pastors are referred to as *under shepherds* (they function under the command of Jesus Christ). Jesus is the *Great Shepherd* of true believers, who have the spiritual identity of sheep (1 Peter 5:1-6, Hebrews 13:20, John 10:27).

Are you a sheep or a goat? Of course you are God's sheep. However, is your daily behaviour similar to that of goats? Are you so stubborn that you refuse to take simple instruction from your pastor or leader? Are you so curious about worldly things while paying little attention to godly things? Do you love gathering with the flock of God at *home fellowship* and *prayer meetings* or you prefer to stay on your own? The difference between sheep and goats lies in *humility and obedience*. Humility is a godly <u>attitude</u> that you embrace by choice. *Don't pray that God will humble you; humility is a command for you to obey!* (1 Peter 5:6)

Prayer: *Almighty and Everlasting God, I rededicate myself to You. I refuse to be a stubborn goat. Help me to honour my pastor. Help me to be teachable! Help me to give high priority to fellowship and prayer meetings, in Jesus' Name.*

September 12
THE LORD'S TABLE

The cup of blessing which we bless, is it not the communion of the blood of Christ? The bread which we break, is it not the communion of the body of Christ? You cannot drink the cup of the Lord and the cup of demons; you cannot partake of the Lord's table and of the table of demons.
— 1 Corinthians 10:16,21

Idolatry is to disregard the Most High as the only true God and to worship any other entity in substitution of Him. Idolatry is sin, and the first commandment in *Exodus 3:20* says that 'You shall have no other gods but Me'. Idols can take many forms. Anything that is competing with the true knowledge of God in your life is an idol. Anything that demands more priority in your life than God is an idol to you. The Bible makes us to understand in *1 Corinthians 10:14-22* that the ancestral gods that some people worship are demon spirits. *You cannot serve two masters, because there is only one true God.* You cannot drink the cup of the Lord and the cup of demons; you cannot partake of the Lord's table and of the table of demons (Luke 16:13).

The *Holy Communion* reminds us that we have willingly entered into a covenant relationship with Christ. In *John 6:53-55*, Jesus said that those who 'eat His flesh' and 'drink His blood' have His life in themselves. *The body of Jesus was broken, so that you can be healed. The blood of Jesus was shed, so that you can be forgiven.* We are to partake of the Lord's table in all sincerity (1 Corinthians 11:23-32).

Confession: *The body of Jesus was broken for me and His blood was shed for me. I have willingly entered into a covenant relationship with Christ. I reject all idolatry! I partake of the Lord's table in all sincerity, in Jesus' Name.*

September 13
HELP IN HIS NAME

**Some *trust* in chariots, and some in horses;
But we will remember the name of the Lord our God.
They have bowed down and fallen; But we have risen and
stand upright.** – Psalm 20:7-8

Have you ever found yourself in a situation where you feel so powerless and helpless? Such situations can make you feel lonely and dejected. However, don't ever forget that you have Jesus Christ, who has promised to never leave nor forsake you. *Even when it seems that all options have failed, God is able to see you through*. All you need do is to call upon the Name of the Lord your God. Ask Him to help you. *Wait upon Him for inspiration and direction*. Make supplication in the Name of Jesus. Say to yourself boldly: *The Lord is my helper; I will not fear* (Hebrews 13:5-6).

Some people put their trust in the arm of flesh. They are confident in their money, skills and personal connections. However, the arm of flesh will fail ultimately. Only God can lift you to stand and remain standing upright. *Psalm 50:14-15* says you are to *offer unto God thanksgiving,* and to *pay your vows to Him*. As you do this, you can be confident to *call upon Him in the day of trouble.* He shall deliver you for He knows that you will honour and glorify Him. Say to yourself: *I have help; my help is in the Name of the Lord.*

**Our help *is* in the name of the Lord,
Who made heaven and earth.** – Psalm 124:8

Prayer: Dear Father, thank You because I can come boldly before You in the Name of Jesus. Thank You because You are my very own Father, and you love me dearly. I receive wisdom and boldness to pray effectively, in Jesus' Name.

September 14
PERFORMANCE AND REWARD

For what profit is it to a man if he gains the whole world, and loses his own soul? Or what will a man give in exchange for his soul? For the Son of Man will come in the glory of His Father with His angels, and then He will reward each according to his works. – Matthew 16:26-27

Have you ever wondered why you have to go through tests and exams, before degrees and certificates are awarded. Why do employees have to go through a probationary period before their employment status is confirmed? A successful probation (test, exam) leads to confirmation (validation, certification). This reflects how God deals with men and angels (Romans 2:5-11, Revelation 22:11-12). *Performance must be tested before rewards are confirmed.* Lucifer failed his supreme test and is damned forever. He had no excuse, for he had beheld and experienced the fullness of God's glory. Adam and Eve also failed their supreme test, due to the deception from Satan, but God in His mercy had foreseen this and also provided a way out to save and restore mankind. It was *pride* that led to the Fall of Satan. God resists the proud but gives grace to the humble. *The antidote to pride is quick repentance and a consistent attitude of submission towards God.* Your lifetime on earth is a time of probation. Don't waste your life! Your performance in life determines your eternal status. Your eternal rewards depend on faith, humility and obedience. *Obedience is the greatest human responsibility.*

Confession: *My performance in life determines my eternal status. I refuse to waste my lifetime on earth. I choose to walk with God in faith, humility and obedience. I refuse to be selfish and stubborn. I choose to live for His glory, daily.*

IT'S TIME TO GET YOUR COPY OF

WALKING WITH GOD DAILY DEVOTIONAL PART FOUR (OCTOBER – DECEMBER)

IT'S TIME TO
GET YOUR COPY OF

WALKING WITH GOD
DAILY DEVOTIONAL
PART FOUR
(OCTOBER – DECEMBER)

September 15
MAN'S RESPONSIBILITY

Therefore submit to God. Resist the devil and he will flee from you. – James 4:7

The greatest asset that God has given to every person is free will: the ability to make choices. You should use that 'free will' to submit to God and to resist the devil. You are to study and meditate on the Word of God daily, because it feeds your spirit and renews your mind. You are to believe the Word concerning your situation, to identify with what the Word says that you are in Christ, and to proclaim it over your situation. You are to claim your healing, supply, deliverance and victory by faith. It is your responsibility to refuse to be worried about anything, to pray regularly in the Spirit, to give thanks in everything, and to rejoice in the Lord always. It is your responsibility to pay your tithes and give offerings as part of your financial partnership with God. It is your responsibility to take corresponding actions in line with your faith, maintain your ground on the Word, and persevere in your faith. It is your responsibility to resist and rebuke the devil. It is your responsibility to take good care of (and to glorify God in) your body.

Note that the devil is a tempter and an attempter. He will try to put anything on anybody. Stand your ground on the Word and don't back off. The devil may roar with adverse circumstances, but you are to stand firm and maintain your ground on the Rock of ages. *When you resist the devil steadfastly, he has to flee from you* (1 Peter 5:8-9).

Prayer: *Heavenly Father, I thank You for the triumphant victory of Christ at the cross of Calvary. I rejoice that I can stand firm in that victory by faith. I refuse to be lazy. Help me to stand my ground on the Word, in Jesus' Name. Amen*

September 16
BLESS THE LORD

Bless the Lord, O my soul;
And all that is within me, *bless* His holy name!
Bless the Lord, O my soul,
And forget not all His benefits.
– Psalm 103:1-2

In many chapters of *the book of Psalms*, the Bible refers to 'blessing the Lord'. What does it mean to 'bless the Lord'? It means to 'praise the Lord'. It means to enter into His gates with thanksgiving and into His courts with praise. Some people think that it is inappropriate for man to bless God. *Is it true that God doesn't need anything from us mere mortals?* In a sense, the answer is: yes, for God is the *All-sufficient One*. However, in another sense, the answer is: no, for God has *free will*, with an implication of desire and choice. *God desires worship and He has chosen man as the medium to fulfil that desire!* (Psalm 34:1, 100:3, 8:4).

Worship is the expression of reverence, adoration, and devotion to an entity. *God wants you to know Him intimately, love Him deeply, honour Him reverently, praise Him abundantly, serve Him faithfully, glorify Him continuously and enjoy Him totally*. You bless the Lord by praising Him for who He is (come into His presence with singing). You bless the Lord that thanking Him for what He has done (forget not all His benefits). You bless the Lord by honouring Him in tithes and offerings (your <u>financial commitment</u> to the Lord is an act of genuine worship).

Confession: *I have confidence in my Heavenly Father. He is El-Shaddai: 'The All-sufficient God'. Bless the Lord, O my soul; and all that is within me, bless His holy name! Bless the Lord, and forget not all His benefits. Glory Hallelujah!*

September 17
JESUS CHRIST IS LORD

And being found in appearance as a man, He humbled Himself and became obedient to the point of death, even the death of the cross. Therefore God also has highly exalted Him and given Him the name which is above every name, that at the name of Jesus every knee should bow, of those in heaven, and of those on earth, and of those under the earth, and that every tongue should confess that Jesus Christ is Lord, to the glory of God the Father. – Philippians 2:8-11

The eternal Word came down from Heaven to do the will of the Father. He left his Heavenly glory and put on the weakness of humanity. He ate as a man, felt tired as a man, slept as a man, worked hard as a man and was tempted as man. He was able to accomplish His mission by embracing an attitude of *Humility* and *Obedience*. This is why Jesus often referred to Himself as the *Son of Man*, for he came to identify with our humanity. Yet, He is also the *Son of God*, for He was incarnated into the virgin womb of Mary by God *the Father* (Hebrews 4:15, John 1: 14).

It was *the Father* who anointed Jesus with the power of the *Holy Spirit*, such that He went about doing good, and healing all who were oppressed of the devil (Acts 10:38). Jesus Christ honoured the Father while on earth. *He was an obedient son like Isaac, even unto death.* Therefore, the Father has also honoured Him as <u>Lord over all creation</u> and has given Him the Name which is above every name in all of existence: *that wonderful and powerful Name of Jesus!*

Prayer: *Thank You Father for Your everlasting love towards me. Thank You for sending Your Son to die for me. Thank You for saving me from spiritual death. Jesus Christ is Lord over all creation, and His Name is wonderful and powerful!*

September 18
AUTHORITY OVER EVIL

Therefore submit to God.
Resist the devil and he will flee from you.
– James 4:7

Certain problems in our lives are the direct work of the devil and his agents. Instead of crying out to God to rebuke the enemy, the Bible says that we are to resist and rebuke the devil ourselves. *Authority over evil belongs to us today because Jesus Christ has already won the victory over death and hell through His death, burial and resurrection.* Jesus Christ is now seated at the Right Hand of the Father and we are seated with Him, far above all principality and power and throne and dominion. *Authority over the devil belongs to us: we are to use it in our situations and circumstances* (Revelation 1:18, Ephesians 1:19-23).

We need to understand that ungodly conditions exist in our lives because we permit them to. *How do we permit them? Because we do nothing about them!* It is not God's responsibility to resist and rebuke the devil for you. He has already given you the authority in Jesus' Name. If you'll resist the devil in faith, he will flee (run away as in flight) from you. The devil has no right to dominate and oppress you. He has no right in your household. *Exercise your authority over evil!* Take the Name of Jesus and <u>break</u> the power of the devil over your life. <u>Command</u> evil forces to cease in their operations against you. <u>Declare</u> your victory over evil in the Name of Jesus. *Hold fast your confession!*

Confession: *I am seated with Christ above all principality and power. I have authority over evil. I refuse to be a victim in life. I break the devil's power and I command evil forces to cease in their operations against me, in Jesus' Name.*

September 19
SEED TO THE SOWER

Now may He who supplies seed to the sower, and bread for food, supply and multiply the seed you have sown and increase the fruits of your righteousness
– 2 Corinthians 9:10

The Lord supplies *seed to the sower* and *bread to the eater* in that order. This means that whatever you receive, first take out your seed (e.g. tithe) and give it to the Lord. *Don't eat your seed* for it is your seed that unlocks your harvest. When you plant your seed by giving, you should plant it in *faith and obedience*, with the expectation of a harvest, because God is faithful to His word and *the scriptures cannot be broken* (Luke 6:38, John 10:35, Genesis 8:22).

Tithing is not the last word in generosity; it's the first. Pay your tithe where you receive spiritual nourishment (e.g. your local church). Give it as a first fruit, as soon as you receive *any income*, lest you're tempted to spend it. Give offerings over and above your tithes. Also give alms or donations to those in need and to charity (Proverbs 19:17). Our Lord Jesus said that *it is more blessed to give than to receive* (Acts 20:35). This refers to all forms of giving (talents, time, energy, resources or money). *Why?* Because giving makes you a blessing to another! Being blessed is not just about having, but also about making good things happen for others. What you make happen for others, God will make happen for you. *A true believer in Christ cannot afford to be stingy or tight-fisted* (Proverbs 11:24-25).

Prayer: Almighty God, thank You for all You have given me. There is nothing I have that I have not received. I refuse to be selfish and stingy. I am loving and generous. I'm a seed-sower and I expect supernatural blessings, in Jesus' Name.

September 20
RESPECT AND APPRECIATION

Let love *be* **without hypocrisy. Abhor what is evil. Cling to what is good.** *Be* **kindly affectionate to one another with brotherly love, in honor giving preference to one another;**
– Romans 12:9-10

Every normal human being wants to be appreciated for the good things they do, and nobody likes to be disrespected. Every true believer in Christ is called to 'walk in God's love'. Walking in love will always overflow into 'respect and appreciation' of others. Some people think love means condoning the evil that men do. *No!* Some are of the impression that those who correct them do not love them. This is not true, for love must be without hypocrisy. *We are to love the sinner but hate the sin.* Love means sacrifice: to seek the best for others, and to bear with them *until they become conformed to the image of the Son* (Romans 8:29). Wives, use the general etiquettes of *respect* applicable to your spoken language to address your husband. *Your respect for your husband must be in word and deed.* Husbands, use the general etiquettes of compassion and affection in your spoken language to address your wife. *Your love for your wife must be in word and deed.* Christian couples should learn to appreciate each other for the little things they do daily. *Appreciation is not activated until it is voiced out!* You have to *say it out* on a regular basis. *Faith comes by hearing* and a wrong confession will always lead to the wrong results (Proverbs 31:26-31, Ephesians 5:33).

Confession: *My life is governed by the Word. My home is a place where the 'grace and truth' of Jesus reigns. I refuse to be selfish! I promote peace and joy in my home by walking in love, with respect and appreciation, in Jesus' Name.*

September 21
NOT YOURS BUT HIS

Behold, children *are* a heritage from the Lord,
The fruit of the womb *is* a reward.
Like arrows in the hand of a warrior,
So *are* the children of one's youth.
— Psalm 127:3-4

Children are a heritage from the Lord! This means that children are a gift from God and they belong to Him. *They are not yours but His.* In this regard, you are the <u>God-appointed custodian</u> of your children, *so that you can train and release them into their God-given destinies*. The best legacy that you can give your children is to <u>train them up in the way of the Lord</u> (Proverbs 22:6, Ephesians 6:4).

Some parents think that loving their children only involves taking them to leisure parks, holidays, restaurants and parties. No! While those things are not necessarily bad, making them your priority in the place of paying attention to the proper upbringing of your children is carelessness and foolishness. Training your children is not just about giving them the best education. This is good in itself, but it can never substitute teaching them to know and walk with God. *Train them to love God!* Lead them by your personal example of <u>diligence</u> in the things of God. *Find wisdom to motivate them towards God!* Start training your children from babyhood. Teach them the Word daily (e.g. Bible stories). *Get them to church meetings!* Love them, pray for them and discipline them. *You cannot afford to fail them!*

Prayer: *Dear Heavenly Father, I thank You for the gift of children. I am the God-appointed custodian of my children. I will train and release them into their God-given destinies. Grant me wisdom to love and train them, in Jesus' Name.*

September 22
THE ANTICHRIST

Let no one deceive you by any means; for *that Day will not come* unless the falling away comes first, and the man of sin is revealed, the son of perdition, who opposes and exalts himself above all that is called God or that is worshiped, so that he sits as God in the temple of God, showing himself that he is God.
– 2 Thessalonians 2:3-4

The man called antichrist is the 'son of perdition'. Those who reject the 'grace and truth' of Jesus Christ will suffer an endurance of the wrath of God under the antichrist: that Satanic man of sin (the beast) who will reign over the world in the tribulation period: the last 7 years of man's rule on the earth. The second half of the tribulation is called the *Great Tribulation* (2 Thessalonians 2:1-12).

Those who have hardened their hearts against the Most High will be deceived into worshipping the antichrist and pledging eternal allegiance to him by taking the *mark of the beast* on their right hands or on their foreheads. No one will be allowed to buy or sell without the mark. Those who worship the beast and receive his mark will be *eternally damned*, for the worship of *the antichrist* is the ultimate form of rebellion against God. The number of the name of the beast (antichrist) is the number of a man: 666. The antichrist and his cohorts will also be used to judge and destroy the false 'apostate' church (that great harlot which had connived with the antichrist to persecute the saints) at this time (Revelations 13:16-18, 17:16-17).

Confession: *The Rapture is the Blessed Hope of true believers in Christ. In the twinkling of an eye, we shall be translated up to Heaven. I will continue to abide faithfully in Christ, and I will not be found wanting when He returns.*

IT'S TIME TO
GET YOUR COPY OF

WALKING WITH GOD
DAILY DEVOTIONAL
PART FOUR
(OCTOBER – DECEMBER)

IT'S TIME TO
GET YOUR COPY OF

WALKING WITH GOD
DAILY DEVOTIONAL
PART FOUR
(OCTOBER – DECEMBER)

September 23
CONTROL YOUR ANGER

"Be angry, and do not sin": do not let the sun go down on your wrath, nor give place to the devil. – Ephesians 4:26-27

A major element of the fruit of the Spirit is self-control. *Uncontrolled anger is not a symbol of strength. Rather, it is a symptom of inner weakness*. We understand in *Proverbs 25:28* that he who has no self-control is like a defenceless city – one without walls. Such a person will be vulnerable to the attacks of Satan through unbelievers and body-ruled Christians. *Uncontrolled anger* and *impatience* are both symptoms of the lack of self-control (Galatians 5:22-23).
Does this mean that all anger is sin? No! There is a difference between selfish anger and holy anger. Every true believer should have a holy anger against sin. We are to hate evil and hold fast to what is good (Romans 12:9).
Anger is not sin until it makes you to walk outside of love and produce evil works. Anger becomes uncontrolled and sinful when it is mixed with bitterness and unforgiveness towards the offender. This is because bitterness will always crave for revenge. *An unforgiving person will fill it difficult to fulfil the greatest commandment (Love)*. For this reason, unforgiveness is a major hindrance to answered prayer. The best way to deal with anger is to 'walk in the Spirit'. Yield to the Spirit by giving up your rights. Don't hold too tightly to any bad feelings. *Hand them over to God, who is* <u>*the Righteous Judge*</u>*, and keep your spirit free of offences and evil* (Ephesians 2:10, Mark 11:25-26, Romans 12:19).

Prayer: *Almighty and Everlasting God, I thank You because the fruit of the Spirit is love and self-control. I have love and self-control inside me. I refuse to be dominated by anger. I am quick to forgive and walk in love, in Jesus' Name. Amen*

September 24
GODLINESS WITH CONTENTMENT

Now godliness with contentment is great gain. For we brought nothing into *this* world, *and it is* certain we can carry nothing out … For the love of money is a root of all *kinds of* evil, for which some have strayed from the faith in their greediness, and pierced themselves through with many sorrows.
– 1 Timothy 6:6-10

Prosperity can be defined as having enough of God's provision to do God's will. It can also be defined as having enough to meet your needs and give to others. However, prosperity is not the same as greed. *A greedy person wants (and keeps wanting) everything for himself.* Greedy people are overcome with an intense desire for acquisition, such that they are willing to lie, cheat or steal in order to get what they want. A greedy person is selfish and covetous; nothing is ever good enough for them. *True prosperity involves thankfulness and a willingness to give back into the kingdom.* Godliness with contentment is great gain!
Some people talk as if they hate money and wealth, but this is not true, otherwise they wouldn't be working for money at all. Money in itself is not evil, for it is God who gives power to get wealth (Deuteronomy 8:18). However, the love of money is the root of all kinds of evil. You have to make sure that money does not become your master. *Your contentment can be measured by your attitude towards giving.* This includes giving praise, thanks, tithes, offerings, donations and alms (Hebrews 13:5, Matthew 6:19-24).

Confession: *I am a child of God and He is my Father. Money is not my master. I refuse to be selfish and greedy. I embrace godliness with contentment. I embrace prosperity with thankfulness and generous giving, in Jesus' Name.*

September 25
DO IT HEARTILY

And whatever you do, do it heartily, as to the Lord and not to men, knowing that from the Lord you will receive the reward of the inheritance; for you serve the Lord Christ.
– Colossians 3:23-24

The right attitude towards Christian service is to 'do it heartily'. Not all service is acceptable to the Lord! A shabby low-quality service will receive little or no reward. *Psalm 100:2* talks about *'serving the Lord with gladness'.* Every true believer is expected *to serve God wholeheartedly!*
In *Matthew 25:14-30,* the Lord Jesus taught about *talents* given to different servants, according to their abilities. *Talents* are opportunities to use our natural and spiritual abilities to serve the Lord. Do you see God as *'harsh, demanding, and unreasonable'*? Are you motivated by fear rather than faith? The servant that refuses to use his God-given talents to serve the Lord is called *'wicked, lazy and worthless'* (Matthew 25:26). What impact can you make for Jesus where you are today? *What can you begin to do in your church, in order to move the work of God forward?*

"Do not lay up for yourselves treasures on earth, where moth and rust destroy and where thieves break in and steal; but lay up for yourselves TREASURES IN HEAVEN, where neither moth nor rust destroys and where thieves do not break in and steal. For where your treasure is, there your heart will be also.
– Matthew 6:19-21

Prayer: Dear Father, thank You for loving me so much that You gave me Your best gift: Jesus Christ. I want to serve You faithfully. Help me to give freely of my money, time, talents, resources and capabilities, in Jesus' Name. Amen.

September 26
GOD OF THIS WORLD

But even if our gospel is veiled, it is veiled to those who are perishing, whose minds the god of this age has blinded, who do not believe, lest the light of the gospel of the glory of Christ, who is the image of God, should shine on them.
– 2 Corinthians 4:3-4

When God created Adam, He gave him the *Title-Deed* of the earth, with full blessing and dominion (Genesis 1:28). However, Adam lost his dominion when he sold out to the devil and committed *High Treason* against God. Therefore, Satan became the *god of this world*. It is therefore no wonder that darkness is prevalent and the world is in such a mess. *Don't ever think that God is running everything in this world. He is not!* Thankfully, He will do so one day (when Jesus Christ returns to reign for 1,000 years).

For now, God's perfect will is only being carried out in the lives of those who surrender to Him. This is why we pray: 'Your Kingdom come, Your will be done on earth as it is in Heaven' (Matthew 6:10). As true believers in Christ, we must remember that although we are in this world, we are not of this world (John 17:16). Jesus has already defeated the devil through His death, burial and resurrection. We (the body) are seated with Christ (the head) at the *Right Hand* of the *Father*, far above all principality and power (Ephesians 1:19-23). Satan's running a lot of things but he's not running us. *We are to dominate him and break his power!* We have authority to do so in the Name of Jesus.

Confession: *I am seated with Christ at the Right Hand of the Father, far above all principality and power. Satan has no right over me. I refuse to be dominated by evil. I break the power of Satan over my life and family, in Jesus' Name.*

September 27
SHINE FOREVER

Those who are wise shall shine
Like the brightness of the firmament,
And those who turn many to righteousness
Like the stars forever and ever. – Daniel 12:3

You were made to live forever! This explains why there is no normal person who wants to die. Many are seeking for immortality on this earth. Although the end of this life is certain, many are trying to establish a legacy that will outlast them on the earth. However, we need to realise that this world itself is passing away. Whatever secular achievements you have will ultimately be <u>superseded or forgotten or wiped out</u> by another generation. This is why our Lord Jesus firmly instructed us in *Matthew 6:19-21* not to lay up our treasures on the earth where they can be destroyed. Instead, we are to lay up treasures in Heaven.

How do you lay up your treasures in Heaven? You do this by investing in the Kingdom of God with your time, skills, money and resources. Don't forget that the purpose of God in creation is <u>worship</u>, and the plan of God in history is <u>redemption</u>. *You achieve immortality in the new earth by your true contributions to the advancement of worship and redemption on this earth.* The Bible tells us that '*he who wins souls is wise*'. <u>You cannot continue to live selfishly.</u> Begin to live for Jesus Christ today. Don't waste your life! *Investing your life into the advancement of the kingdom will help to turn many to righteousness!* (Proverbs 11:30)

Prayer: *Dear Father in Heaven, I rededicate myself to You. Help me to invest my time, skills, money and resources into the advancement of Your Kingdom on this earth. I want to shine forever in the world to come, in Jesus' Name. Amen.*

September 28
SUPPLICATION AND INTERCESSION

Therefore I exhort first of all that supplications, prayers, intercessions, *and* giving of thanks be made for all men, for kings and all who are in authority, that we may lead a quiet and peaceable life in all godliness and reverence. For this *is* good and acceptable in the sight of God our Savior, who desires all men to be saved and to come to the knowledge of the truth. – 1 Timothy 2:1-4

What is supplication? It is a heartfelt, fervent and earnest request (James 5:16-18). You present your case before God using His Word. *God respects you <u>standing as a man on His Word</u>.* God gave man dominion over the earth and God needs the cooperation of man to rule on the earth. *What is intercession?* It is 'standing in the gap' against judgement (Ezekiel 22:30-31). It means standing in the place of prayer to execute the divine will in terms of salvation, healing and deliverance. *God's will cannot be done on earth until man agrees and cooperates with God* (Luke 11:2, 2 Peter 3:9). When the will of man cooperates with the will of God (His Word and His purposes), great miracles become possible. We enter into this cooperation with God through prayer. *We are His royal priesthood on the earth. We are to make supplication and intercession on behalf of <u>all</u> men.* We are to pray for <u>all</u> who are in authority, so that we can have the peace needed for evangelism. *We are to intercede for the salvation of souls and evangelise, because God <u>desires</u> <u>all</u> men to be saved!* (1 Peter 2:9, 2 Corinthians 5:18-20)

Confession: *I desire that God's will be done on earth as it is in Heaven. Therefore, I give myself to prayer continuously. I make supplication and intercession on behalf of all men. I intercede for souls and I preach the gospel, in Jesus' Name.*

September 29
NOTHING IN ME

**If you love Me, keep My commandments.
I will no longer talk much with you, for the ruler of this world is
coming, and he has nothing in Me.** – John 14:15,30

*The Bible talks about Satan being the ruler of this world. He
presides over the darkness of this age.* However, he has
only but a short time left <u>to do his worst</u> before the *King of
Glory* (Jesus Christ) steps in to reign for 1,000 years. For
now, Christ must reign on the earth through us, for we are
part of His body. *On His way to the Cross, Jesus declared
that the devil has nothing in Him.* This means nothing in
common and nothing that belongs to him. *Does Satan have
anything in you? Have you made room for him in your life?*
Is there anything in your life that you are holding on to,
ever so tightly? Is there something you can't let go of, for
the sake of Jesus? Are there habits (even good ones) that
you can't do without? Is there anything in your life that
comes before God? All these can become a foothold for
the devil. *It is important not to allow Satan to get an
advantage over you!* (Ephesians 4:27, 2 Corinthians 2:11)
Examine yourself: is there something of the devil in you?
Are you dealing with your spouse in selfishness? Are you
inconsiderate of the needs of others? *Do you talk harshly
or carelessly?* Are you addicted to TV or the internet? *Are
you consuming alcohol?* Is there anger and unforgiveness
in you? Whatever holds you bound will hinder your faith
from working. *Make sure that Satan has nothing in you!*

Prayer: *Almighty God, thank You because I am a member
of the body of Christ. Jesus Christ is my King, and Satan has
nothing in me. I refuse to be dominated by anything. I
refuse to be addicted to anything. I am free in Jesus' Name.*

September 30
ANGELS ON GUARD

The angel of the Lord encamps all around those who fear Him, And delivers them. – Psalm 34:7

The holy angels of God are ministering spirits. They are divine messengers sent forth to minister for true believers. Angels are mighty in strength and they God's counsel, in line with His Word. *Psalm 34:7* shows us that angels are *on guard* around those who fear God. In *Daniel 6*, we read the story of the prophet Daniel, a man who feared God and refused to take part in idolatry. As a result, he was cast into the den of lions. However, God sent His angel to shut the lions' mouths, so they could not hurt him. The angel delivered Daniel from impending death (Hebrews 1:14).

2 Kings 6:8-23 tells us the story of the prophet Elisha, when his city was surrounded by an army of Syrian raiders. His servant panicked when he saw this great army with horses and chariots. However, Elijah said: *"Do not fear, for those who are with us are more than those who are with them."* When the spiritual eyes of the young servant were opened, he saw that their mountain was protected by a greater host of angels, with horses and chariots of fire.

Psalm 91:11 shows us that angels are *sent forth to keep us* in all our ways. They are watching over those who honour God, to keep their lives from being crushed. It is crucial to understand that the ministry of angels is <u>severely hindered by disobedience</u>. *As you walk in true obedience, you should confidently expect angels to guard and minister for you!*

Confession: *Angels are in charge over me. They protect me. They minister for me. Satan, take your hands off my life, my family, and my finances. Go forth ministering spirits, cause divine supply to come in for me, in Jesus' Name.*

DECISION

Prayer for Salvation:

Dear God, I come to you today.
I acknowledge that I was born with a sinful nature, I have lived in rebellion against You, and I cannot save myself.
I believe that Your eternal Word came down in human flesh as Jesus Christ, the Son of God.
I believe that He died on the cross as the eternal sacrifice for Sin.
I repent of Sin and I accept His eternal sacrifice for my sins today.
I receive Jesus Christ into my heart as my Saviour, and I confess with my mouth that Jesus Christ is my Lord.
I choose to trust and obey Him, and to live for Him every day.
From now on, I will fulfil my design-purpose of worship as I go through life in faith and obedience to Christ, until I see Him face-to-face.
Thank You for saving me.
I am now born-again.
I'm a child of God and God is my Father.
I'm a winner.
Glory to God! Hallelujah! Amen!

Name:_____

Date:_____

ABOUT THE AUTHOR

Dr Ben Awoseyila is the founding pastor of Healing Springs Church, Basingstoke, UK. *Healing Springs* is a loving, multicultural Pentecostal church, founded in October 2012, with a mission of *equipping you to live victoriously*.

Dr Ben obtained his B.Sc. degree (1st Class) in Electronics and Electrical Engineering from the Obafemi Awolowo University, Ile-Ife, Nigeria in 1998. He also obtained both M.Sc. (with Distinction) and Ph.D. degrees in Mobile and Satellite Communications from the University of Surrey, Guildford, UK, in 2005 and 2008 respectively. He has worked in research and teaching at the University of Surrey for several years, and he is passionate about teaching his subject area.

Ben is happily married to his beloved wife: Jummy, who co-pastors alongside with him. They are blessed with three 'wonderful and energetic' boys, who love the Lord.

Pastor Ben is passionate about helping people solve their problems, inspiring them to walk with God, and teaching them divine truths for victorious living.

If this book has blessed you, you can share your story with us and/or send free-will donations to support our mission and/or visit us at Healing Springs Church UK.

Contact:
ben_aab@me.com

Donate via Paypal:
ben_aab@me.com

Visit our Website:
www.HealingSpringsChurch.org

OTHER BOOKS BY THE AUTHOR

1. **The Purpose of Life: Your Questions Answered,** Available for purchase on Amazon, *March 2014.*

2. **Walking with God: Daily Devotional Part One,** Available for purchase on Amazon, *November 2014.*

3. **Walking with God: Daily Devotional Part Two,** Available for purchase on Amazon, *March 2015.*

4. **Walking with God: Daily Devotional Part Three,** Available for purchase on Amazon, *May 2015.*

5. **Walking with God: Daily Devotional Part Four,** Available for purchase on Amazon, *August 2015.*

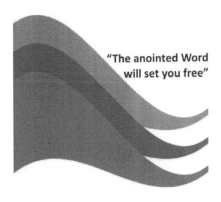

"The anointed Word will set you free"

Published by Springs International

10912277R00066

Printed in Great Britain
by Amazon.co.uk, Ltd.,
Marston Gate.